Souvenir Guide

Contents

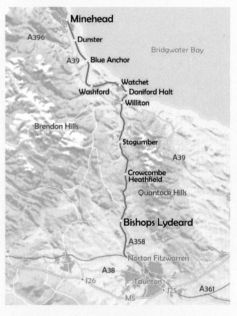

Printed and bound in Ceská Republika

First published in 2012 by:
The West Somerset Railway PLC
The Railway Station
Minehead   Tel/Fax: 01643 704996
Somerset   email: info@west-somerset-railway.co.uk
TA24 5BG   Website: www.west-somerset-railway.co.uk

Follow us on Twitter: http://twitter.com/WSomRailway
Find us on Facebook – West Somerset Railway
Watch us on www.youtube.com/wsrail

Text: Written by John Simms and contributors
        © West Somerset Railway PLC
Maps © Stephen Edge
Layout and design: © Silver Link Publishing Ltd

Photos: © *WSR Collection* unless otherwise credited
The producers of this book have, where possible, credited those responsible for taking the photographs in this guide. Where photographs have been submitted to the West Somerset Railway PLC for use in publications and we have been unable to ascertain the name of the photographer, they have been credited as *WSR Collection*. If we have included but not credited you with any photographs that you have submitted, please supply us with your details and we will endeavour to correct the omission in future editions.

In association with:
Silver Link Publishing Ltd
The Trundle
Ringstead Road
Great Addington   Tel/Fax: 01536 330588
Kettering   email: sales@nostalgiacollection.com
Northants NN14 4BW   Website: www.nostalgiacollection.com

Opposite: 'Mogul' 2-6-0 No 9351 arrives at Williton with an appropriate set of 'chocolate and cream' carriages. *Michael H. C. Baker*

Great Britain's
Heritage Railways

Above: Ex-LNER 'A4' 4-6-2 No 4468 *Mallard* stands at York heading the 'Mallard 88' Settle & Carlisle rail tour on 17 July 1988.

Above right: For a time the only steam loco granted permission to run over BR metals after the 'end of steam' was ex-LNER 'A3' No 4472 *Flying Scotsman*, seen here racing through Northallerton, on the East Coast Main Line north of York, in September 1975, re-enacting the legendary King's Cross to Edinburgh service.

Right: During the summer of 1974 'V2' 2-6-2 No 4771 *Green Arrow* races up the bank towards Ulverston, between Carnforth and Barrow, one of the five routes opened to steam in 1972.

Great Britain's Heritage Railways

The rise of the railway preservation movement

David Mather

Silver Link Publishing Ltd

For my wife Mair, whose patience and support have made this work possible, and my son Andrew, who accompanied us without question.

First published in 2012

British Library Cataloguing in Publication Data

A catalogue record for this book is available from the British Library.

ISBN 978 1 85794 406 8 (West Somerset Railway Edition)
ISBN 978 1 85794 407 5 (Severn Valley Railway Edition)
ISBN 978 1 85794 411 2

Please note: further editions in preparation, please check back cover for specific edition ISBN details.

Silver Link Publishing Ltd
The Trundle
Ringstead Road
Great Addington
Kettering
Northants NN14 4BW

Tel/Fax: 01536 330588
email: sales@nostalgiacollection.com
Website: www.nostalgiacollection.com

Printed and bound in the Czech Republic

Please note: Due to the variable and seasonal nature of both opening times and train times and services on heritage railways, those intending to visit/travel should check availability with the railway or centre direct in advance.

Contents

Preface

L ike so many of my generation, raised in the era of steam-hauled trains, the events culminating in August 1968 seemed literally like the end of the line for standard-gauge steam on the railways of the UK.

In the year prior to the end of steam on BR, periodicals such as *The Railway Magazine* and *Railway World* listed the last withdrawals of the surviving steam locomotives. Totalling about 100 casualties per month, mainly from the London Midland Region, these lists included the few remaining 'Jubilees', line after line of 'Black 5s', strings of ex-LMS 8Fs, BR Standard Class 5s by the dozen, the last of the mighty 9F 2-10-0s, and the only surviving 'Pacifics' to grace our tracks – the hardy 'Britannias'.

The decision had been made. Steam was finished. Our railways needed to be modernised. Diesel and electric power were the future. The steam age had served us well, but now we must look forward and put the past where it belonged – in history. Normal steam-hauled services therefore ended on 3 August 1968, yet even from the following day the first of several 'Steam Specials' were running, hauled by 'Black 5s', including Nos 44781, 44871 45017 and 45305, 'Britannia' 'Pacific' No 70013 *Oliver Cromwell* or BR Standard 4-6-0 No 73069, until the famous 'last run' on 11 August of that year banished steam to private collections and museums. It is amazing to reflect that locos such as No 70000 *Britannia* were a mere 15 years old when withdrawn in 1966, and that the last steam locomotive built for BR, 9F No 92220 *Evening Star*, had only five years of service before her withdrawal in 1965. Mercifully, there were at this time those whose love of steam railways went far beyond that of the teenage trainspotter – men of vision who refused to let the tide of modernisation sweep the steam locomotive into oblivion, who saw a part of the British way of life disappearing, and decided to do something about it.

When Alan Pegler decided to take his *Flying Scotsman* to America, the only remaining steam-operated service left in British Rail's tender care was the 1ft 11½in-gauge line out of Aberystwyth – the summertime-only tourist run to the waterfalls at Devil's Bridge. The Vale of Rheidol Railway blossomed to form one of the mainstays of the group that would become known as 'The Great Little Trains of Wales', but that was some years in the future. For now, the stirrings of the devoted steam fans were already awakening in others the possibility that preserved steam railways might fill the void, especially as those already up and running, namely the Bluebell and the Dart Valley, were successfully offering steam-hauled rides through pleasant countryside to an ever more appreciative audience.

September 1968, one month on from the end of steam on British Railways, found me leaving my home town of Bolton, Lancashire. The area had been the last outpost of steam haulage on our network, and now it was gone. It was an opportune moment for me to move on too. My other great love, biology and wildlife generally, led me to accept a place to read for a degree at Birmingham University, which would ultimately steer me into a career in science teaching, initially in Wolverhampton, but later back in the North (albeit on the other side of the Pennines) in York.

My passion for steam locomotives lived on, and although the salary of a newly qualified teacher in 1972 was far from generous, it did allow me to travel in search of steam once more. So, from my base in Staffordshire, in the heart of the industrial Black Country, I was drawn first to rural Shropshire and in particular to Bridgnorth, home of the Severn Valley Railway. Weekends were coming back to life again…

Who was organising this fight-back? Where would steam live on?

The world's first preserved railway was the Talyllyn in Mid Wales, which opened for business way back in 1951, in the days when steam still held sway on the nation's rails. This 2ft 3in-gauge railway was saved from closure by a group of enthusiasts who, in 1950, stepped in when the slate quarries that had provided the bulk of the railway's business closed in 1948, threatening the lifting of the track and the sale of the land.

The newly acquired preserved line was an instant success, boasting as it did a demanding start from Towyn station on a gradient of 1 in 10, followed by about 7 miles of uphill running through beautiful countryside towards the slate-mining districts in the hills around Abergynolwyn and Nant Gwernol.

This profitable enterprise was to serve as an inspiration to other would-be preservationists the length and breadth of Britain, and eight years later the first standard-gauge (4ft 8½in) preserved railway was up and running, the Bluebell Railway in Kent, a trail-blazer that so many others would follow.

For me, an Open Day at BR's Cricklewood Depot in July 1969 raised a glimmer of hope that maybe there might be a softening of BR's anti-steam policy, when 'Black 5' No 5428, soon after to be named *Eric Treacy*, 'Jubilee' No 5593 *Kolhapur* and 'Castle' No 7029 *Clun Castle* took turns to haul visitors up and down a short stretch of track. We lived in hope!

Introduction: preserved steam on the main line since 1968

THE FIVE ROUTES

The early 1970s proved to be a turning point for preserved steam, when Richard Marsh was appointed Chairman of BR in 1971. Himself a steam fan, an early step was to arrange the first trial run of the 'Return to Steam' tours in October of that year. The ban imposed from August 1968 was lifted partially, as ex-GWR 'King' Class 4-6-0 No 6000 *King George V* became only the second steam loco to be allowed to run on BR's lines, the other having been Alan Pegler's famous *Flying Scotsman*, by heading a week of 'experimental' excursions from Hereford, taking in Birmingham, London and Swindon. *KGV* was restored at the expense of H. P. Bulmer Ltd, and was an exhibit on that company's private railway in Hereford until she was passed for working excursions between Shrewsbury and Newport in 1971. These 'Cider Trains' were composed partly of preserved Pullman coaches painted up in Bulmer's own livery, and also included 'Aquila', built in 1951 especially for use by the Royal Family and visiting heads of state. They carried with them the hopes and dreams of all steam railway enthusiasts, that should they be deemed successful, they might pave the way for a relaxation or possibly even a lifting of BR's steam ban.

The response from the steam-starved public was overwhelming. Crowds flocked to the lineside and to every station, proving to the sceptics that the draw of steam was becoming more powerful than ever. These events were a major triumph for all involved in the embryonic steam preservation movement and proved to be major stepping-stone towards the wider acceptance of steam power to haul trains again over BR routes, leading as they did to the permanent lifting of the ban and a green light for more locomotives to take to the rails. The success of the 'trial tours' by No 6000 laid bare the 'insurmountable problems' that had previously been cited as the justification for the ban, namely coal and water supplies, availability of steam crews and the reliability of the aging steam locomotives. 1972 saw the first steam-hauled routes become authorised, with 12 trips in the long-awaited 'Return to Steam' programme, sanctioned by BR.

The 1972 agreement permitted steam specials to run over five main-line routes – Birmingham-Didcot, Newcastle-Carlisle, York-

A Great Western and London & North Western Joint Lines warning to trespassers notice dating from 1885, alongside the line near Shrewsbury in 1972.

In 1974 ex-GWR 'King' No 6000 *King George V* is at the forefront of the main-line steam revival. She is seen here at Shrewsbury in charge of 'The Midlander' rail tour, featuring the beautifully presented Pullman coach, 'Aquila'.

Scarborough, Newport-Shrewsbury and Carnforth-Barrow – providing a total of about 300 miles of available track. Locos passed for these routes included, from the old GWR, Nos 4079 *Pendennis Castle*; 6998 *Burton Agnes Hall*, 7029 *Clun Castle* and 6000 *King George V*; ex-LMS 'Jubilee' Nos 5593 *Kolhapur* and 5596 *Bahamas*, together with half a dozen or so 'Black 5s'; from the LNER, 'A4' 'Pacifics' Nos 4498 *Sir Nigel Gresley* and 60019 *Bittern*, and 'A2' 'Pacific' No 532 *Blue Peter*; while 'Merchant Navy' Class No 35028 *Clan Line* carried the flag for the old Southern Railway. BR itself was to be represented by 9F 2-10-0 92203 *Black Prince* and Class 4 4-6-0 No 75029 *The Green Knight*, which, with the addition of other less imposing classes, gave a total of 23 locomotives named as available for consideration for main-line running.

Routes added in 1973 included Kyle of Lochalsh-Inverness, Filey-Hull, Carnforth-Leeds via Keighley, Barrow-Sellafield, Oxford-Hereford and Tyseley-Stratford. Though steam specials were limited to the months of April to June and September and October, the number organised was double that of the previous year and plans were afoot to seek authorisation for cross-country charters linking designated lines and taking locos further afield from their home areas. By 1974, and by popular demand, this list had expanded greatly and the route miles made available had increased to 1,000, and more were being planned.

THE 'BARRY PROJECT'

Most scrap dealers who bought locos from BR in large numbers cut them up immediately, but Woodham Brothers' policy of dealing with wagons first allowed the company to eventually sell the locos for an average £4,000 to enthusiasts, compared with a figure of half that amount that they had cost. It was as a result of the 1955 Modernisation Plan that Dai Woodham became a major player in the steam preservation movement, as the legendary scrapyard began to receive an apparently never-ending supply of material as British Railways sought to reduce its wagon fleet from 1.25 million to 600,000, and to scrap 16,000 steam locomotives. In the first instance the 'wagons first' policy had nothing to do with preserving steam locos – rather that wagons were easier to dispose of and there was a vast number of them. Also, if a slack period did come along, the locomotives were a useful resource in reserve.

At first, when the locomotives were still mostly complete, moving them was relatively simple. BR would supply a diesel and brake-van and, after inspection, the loco would be towed away to the purchaser's site. However, problems with neglected axle-boxes running hot resulted in a ban on movements by rail in 1976, and thereafter all locomotives had to be transported by road. As time passed, and the elements took their toll, the task of restoring the later purchases became more daunting, as many fittings were missing, especially anything in brass, copper or bronze, and major tasks such as re-tubing would require further investment running into several more thousands of pounds. Woodham's early policy of allowing purchasers to remove parts from similar types of locos to make up a 'spare parts kit', provided that the 'donors' were not themselves restored, had compounded this problem. Added to this, illegal 'trophy hunting' and increasing theft forced the yard's owners to impose a total ban on any removal of 'extra' material from the site from 1981.

It was in October 1973 that the Urie S15 Preservation Group published its first 'Barry List', a catalogue of the nearly 300 locomotives withdrawn by BR during the 1960s and sent to the vast scrapyard of Woodham Brothers at Barry Dock, South Wales. This and subsequent editions served not only as sad reminders of former glory days but also provided a further wake-up call to all those involved in the steam preservation movement. In fact, since 1968 the Association of Railway Preservation Societies had been growing from strength to strength and the number of 'rescues' from scrapyards such as Woodham's was gaining momentum.

By the time the Second Edition was published in June 1975, the sad ranks of derelict locos not yet 'torched' still totalled 150, with cutting up due to start in earnest at the end of August of that year and estimated to take up to two years. For the growing number of railway preservation societies the race was therefore on to rescue any that could feasibly be restored and to delay the cutter's torch as

The images in this section have been kindly contributed by Gary Thornton who visited the yards in April 1981.

SIX BELLS JUNCTION

Gary is the webmaster of the popular and informative Six Bells Junction website which features rail tour records stretching back to the 1800s – well worth a visit at:

www.sixbellsjunction.co.uk

Stanier's LMS taper boiler design is represented here by 'Black 5' 4-6-0 No 44901 on the left of the three-loco line-up. Unfortunately the identity of the two other locomotives was not recorded.

Built in 1926 at Swindon works, 0-6-2T No 5668 ended its days in BR service at nearby Barry shed, so it was but a short trip to the Woodhams yards. It is een here on 4 April 1981 some 20 years after withdrawal. The loco is now in private ownership and underrgoing restoration on the Pontypool & Blaenavon Railway.

long as possible. Luckily for all concerned in the steam rescue and restoration world, Woodham's also had major contracts for the cutting up of other scrap vehicles, notably the railway wagons, so many of the locos were reprieved and precious time gained for the raising of funds for the purchase of survivors.

The Sixth Edition of the list (August 1981) noted that, to date, a total of 135 locomotives from Barry had been or were being restored, with a further 78 still held in the yard, of which 34 were reserved and a further 11 sold and awaiting removal to their new homes. The total number of locomotives broken

The first of 200 locos of the '5600' Class designed by Charles B. Collett for work in the Welsh Valleys was introduced by the GWR in 1924. No 6634 was one of the second batch introduced in 1927. Now owned by Pete Waterman, No 6634 is currently undergoing restoration at the workshops of Severn Valley Railway Engineering Services.

up at Woodham Brothers in the period up to 1980 was 84, the overwhelming majority of which were during the period 1959 to 1973, but in the summer of 1980 scrappings were resumed (albeit on a temporary basis due to lack of other work), so the figure for locos broken up passed the 100 mark. Much of the praise for coordinating the purchase of the locos remaining at Barry is due to the Barry Steam Locomotive Action Group, started in February 1979 and incorporated into the National Railway Preservation Campaign soon afterwards under the leadership of Robert Adley MP, with aims to survey the remaining locos in order to ascertain their condition and to a put Woodham Brothers in touch with potential clients, thereby allowing informed decisions regarding the future of the locomotives to be made.

Ex LMS 4F 0-6-0 No 43924 – withdrawn in July 1965, interred in the Barry scrapyard in October of that year, and incidentally the only ex-Midland Railway loco in the yard, as ex-'3835' Class No 3924 – became the first loco to be 'saved' when she was bought for preservation in September 1968 by the Midland 4F Preservation Society, after the short stay of only 2 years 11 months. She was later moved to work successfully at her new home on the Keighley & Worth Valley Railway. By October 1987 nearly 200 more had followed suit. Of these, the majority were former GWR locos, which included 11 'Halls', six 'Modified Halls', eight 'Manors', five 'Castles' and two 'Kings'. From the old LMS the list included two 'Jubilees', six 'Black 5s' and six 8F 2-8-0s, while from the Southern came no fewer than 28 'Pacifics' made up of ten 'Merchant Navy', ten 'West Country' and eight 'Battle of Britain' locomotives. Only one loco represented the LNER, being 'B1' 4-6-0 No 61264, while ex-BR locos included seven 9F 2-10-0s, four BR Class 5 4-6-0s and, most significantly, BR's one and only 8P 'Pacific' No 71000 *Duke of Gloucester*. Among the famous classes represented above were locos destined to become torch-bearers for the preservation movement in years

BR Standard Class 4MT 2-6-4T No 80150 is seen languishing in a long line at Barry on 4 April 1981. Built at Brighton works in 1957, this loco served BR for just 8 years before withdrawal in 1965. Clearly marked for intended preservation by the Avon Valley Railway, the loco departed, first in 1988 to the Bute Road site of the Vale of Glamorgan Railway Company, then in 1997 to their site at Barry, just a short distance from its resting place seen above. However, as this book was going to press No 80150 was moved to the Mid Hants Railway where restoration is already getting under way.

The pride of the Great Western Railway, the 'King' Class 4-6-0, once numbered 30 locomotives. The Western Region of British Railways continued the tradition, rostering them on 'The Cornish Riviera', 'The Bristolian' and other top-line expresses. Perhaps surprisingly three of the class survive:
No 6000 *King George V*
No 6023 *King Edward II*
No 6024 *King Edward I*
Here on 4 April 1981 No 6023 is seen at Barry with clear signs of work having started on a restoration that has taken over 30 years to complete. No 6023 is now back on the main line and is owned by and based at the Great Western Society at Didcot.

to come, including 'Jubilee' No 45690 *Leander*, 'West Country' Class No 34092 *City of Wells*, 'Castle' No 5043 *Earl of Mount Edgcumbe* and 'King' No 6023 *King Edward II*.

Many 'rescues' took between 10 and 20 years to accomplish, though the longest sentence served by any loco before release from Barry was 25 years 1 month, from May 1961 to June 1986, by ex-GWR '4575' Class 2-6-2T No 5552, which was eventually bought in very poor condition by the Bodmin & Wenford Railway Trust and ultimately restored to its former glory to grace its line through the beautiful countryside of the Duchy of Cornwall. Sister loco No 5553 became the last steam locomotive to leave Woodham Brothers' scrapyard in January 1990, when she was saved for the West Somerset Railway and subsequently also restored to full working order.

Left: Bulleid light 'Paciific' 'West Country' Class 4-6-2 No 34028 *Eddystone* is seen in a very sorry-looking state on 4 April 1981 but the messages daubed upon her gave rise for hope that one day she would be removed for restoration and turn her wheels again!

Determination, hard work and enthusiasm succeeded once again and No 34028 moved under her own power on The Swanage Railway on 4 October 2003.

The full list of locomotives at Barry on 4 April 1981 according to Gary's records was:

2807 2859 (2861) 2873 2874 2885 3802 3803 3814 (3845) 3850 3855 3862 4115 4247 4248 4253 4270 4277 4953 4979 5199 (5227) 5526 5538 (5539) 5552 (5553) 5668 (5952) 5967 5972 6023 6634 6686 6984 7200 (7229) 7821 7828 7903 7927 9629 9682 30499 30825 30830 34007 34010 34016 34028 34053 34058 (34070) 34072 34073 35006 35009 35010 35011 35022 (35025) 35027 42859 44123 44901 45163 45293 45337 45491 47406 48173 48305 48518 48624 73096 73156 75079 76077 76084 78059 80072 80097 80098 80104 80150 92207 92219 92245

(Bracketed numbers were ones identified afterwards from records of locos in yard at time of visit, tying in with unidentified locos seen).

Below: Believe it or not Urie 'S15' Class 4-6-0 No 30499 has also departed and is undergoing restoration by the Urie Locomotive Society at Ropley on the Mid Hants Railway. Not surprisingly this is a long-term project, but one day...

Rail 150 Tour

1825
1975

A journey into yesterday

RAIL 150: THE GRAND STEAM CAVALCADE

The year 1975 stood out as a landmark in the annals of steam as celebrations for the 150th anniversary of the opening of the Stockton & Darlington Railway culminated on 31 August with the 'Rail 150 Steam Cavalcade' at Shildon, and the opening of the new National Railway Museum in York on 27 September.

Myself and a few friends joined the masses of enthusiasts assembled from near and far, lining the 4-mile cavalcade route from Shildon to Heighington. This was where it had all begun a century and a half before. This was where George Stephenson had launched *Locomotion* on a world that knew nothing of the concept of a railway, so it was fitting that during the opening ceremony in Shildon on 25 August ex-LMS 'Black 5' No 4767 should be named *George Stephenson* by William Whitelaw, MP for Penrith and the Borders and grandson of Mr William Whitelaw, Chairman of the LNER in 1925 – the year that a previous exhibition had taken place to mark the centenary of the Stockton & Darlington Railway. The naming was doubly significant, as Stanier's loco No 4767, though itself a member of a class of 842, was the only one to be fitted experimentally with valve gear operated by 'Stephenson's link motion'.

The scene was bathed in warm sunshine – much relief after the rain of

Leading the way is the replica of George Stephenson's *Locomotion*, constructed during apprentice training programmes in local engineering firms and towing a caldron wagon and a Stockton & Darlington passenger coach.

The National Coal Board's 0-6-0 saddle tank No 2502/7 was one of many commissioned by the Ministry of Supply to ease the shortage of locomotives available as a result of the Second World War and built by the Hunslet Engine Company of Leeds in 1943 to a ruggedly simple yet economic standard design of shunter.

the previous day – as the combined whistles of more than 30 locomotives signalled the start of this once-in-a-lifetime cavalcade, led by a replica of *Locomotion*, the original being a museum piece not able to be steamed. Pulling a Stockton & Darlington coach, she was greeted by thunderous applause as her crew, doffing immaculate top hats, waved enthusiastically to the cheering crowds.

The evolution of the steam locomotive passed before our eyes on that glorious Sunday, each gleaming example being met with warm appreciation, drowning out the sound of countless camera shutters keenly recording this unique spectacle.

These two locos are now earning their keep on the North Yorkshire Moors Railway. NER Class 'T2' 0-8-0 No 2238 was one of a class of 120 heavy freight locos built at Darlington from 1913, while NER Class 'P3' 0-6-0 No 2392 was built in 1923, also at Darlington Works.

LNER Class 'K1' 2-6-0 No 2005 is now restored to her original 'apple green' livery by the North Eastern Locomotive Preservation Group.

Caledonian Railway Class '439' 0-4-4 tank No 419 was built in Glasgow in 1907.

LNER Class 'D49/1' 4-4-0 No 246 *Morayshire* was built at Darlington in 1928 to haul express passenger trains, and was withdrawn in 1961.

GWR 0-6-0 pannier tank No 7752 of the '57XX' Class was built by the North British Locomotive Company in Glasgow in 1930, and since retirement her home has been the Birmingham Railway Museum, Tyseley.

GWR 'Manor' 4-6-0 No 7808 *Cookham Manor* was restored superbly by the Great Western Society at Didcot. She is one of the nine members of her class of 30 built between 1938 and 1950 to have survived.

Continuing the Great Western theme is 4-6-0 'Modified Hall' No 6960 *Raveningham Hall*, built at Swindon in 1944 and rescued from Barry scrapyard, she later resided at Steamtown, Carnforth, where her restoration was carried out. Only seven of her class of 71 survive.

Right: LNER 'V2' Class 2-6-2 No 4771 was built at Doncaster in 1936 and named *Green Arrow* to head up the company's new express freight service of the same name.

Left: LNER Class 'B1' 4-6-0 No 1306 carries the name *Mayflower*, originally borne by sister loco No 61379 to commemorate the Pilgrim Fathers. Built in 1948, No 1306 later resided at Steamtown, Carnforth. She is the only surviving member of her class of 184 built between 1936 and 1944 and is now part of the National Collection.

Below left: LMS 8F 2-8-0 No 8233 belongs to a class introduced from 1935. This Stanier taper-boiler design of heavy freight loco originally totalled 849, though many were requisitioned directly by the War Department so never carried LMS numbers. No 8233 was one of several sent to serve in the Middle East in 1941, but was lucky enough to survive the experience and return home in peacetime to continue working on BR. She now adorns the Severn Valley Railway. Eight members of the class are preserved in this country, but more may still be in existence overseas, notably in Turkey.

Below right: Continuing the War Department theme, 2-10-0 No 600 *Gordon* is seen hauling London Transport Departmental electric locomotive No 12 *Sarah Siddons*, by now a test vehicle for LT. Carrying the tender initials of the Longmoor Military Railway, a British military railway in Hampshire built by Royal Engineers from 1903 in order to train soldiers on railway construction and operations, *Gordon* was named there in honour of the RE's most famous general, Charles Gordon ('Gordon of Khartoum'), and was the last steam loco owned by the British Army. When the LMR closed in 1969, *Gordon* was preserved on the Severn Valley Railway and entered service there in 1973. Three other members of her class of 150 survive.

One of only four British survivors of her class of 35, LNER 'A4' Class 4-6-2 No 4498 *Sir Nigel Gresley* was named after the company's Chief Mechanical Engineer and designer of many famous classes of LNER locos; it is seen here hauling Great Northern Railway 'A1' Class No 1. In 1938 'A4' No 4468 *Mallard* attained the world speed record for a steam locomotive of 126.4mph, which is still unbeaten.

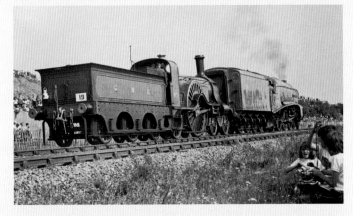

A clearer view of Patrick Stirling's former East Coast 'flyer' No 1 behind No 4498. No 1 took part in the legendary 'Races to the North' in 1888 and 1895 and was also in the 1925 S&D Centenary Procession. After working special trains in the 1930s she was retired to the National Railway Museum.

Following is perhaps the most famous of them all, 'A3' Class 4-6-2 No 4472 *Flying Scotsman*, towing NER Class '901' 2-4-0 No 910. This Gresley loco is the only survivor from a class of 79 locomotives.

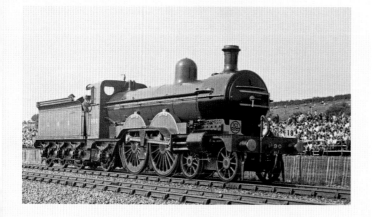

Great Northern Railway Class 'C1' 4-4-2 No 990 *Henry Oakley* was built in 1898 and named after the then General Manager of the GNR; she was the first 4-4-2 tender locomotive to run in this country.

LNWR 'Precedent' Class 2-4-0 No 790 *Hardwicke* also took part in the 'Races to the North' and is, like *Henry Oakley*, a National Railway Museum loco.

Midland Railway 4-4-0 'Compound' No 1000 was built at Derby in 1902 and worked for almost 50 years on express passenger services. She also is part of the collection based at the National Railway Museum.

Now some classic Stanier LMS designs. 'Jubilee' Class 4-6-0 No 5690 *Leander* was rescued from Barry scrapyard and restored at Derby Works before taking up residence at the Dinting Railway Centre near Manchester. Four members of this class of 191 locos survive.

'Princess Royal' Class 4-6-2 No 6201 *Princess Elizabeth* was, like *Leander*, built at Crewe Works. She became a record-setter, with her times for the 401 miles between London and Glasgow in 1936 remaining unbeaten until after the end of the steam era. One other member of this small class of 12 survives, sister loco No 6203 *Princess Margaret Rose.*

LMS Class 5MT 4-6-0 No 4767 is one of the ubiquitous 'Black 5s', of which 842 were built between 1934 and 1950. Named *George Stephenson* at the opening of these celebrations, this loco was built at Crewe Works in 1947 and now graces the tracks of the North Yorkshire Moors Railway. Eighteen 'Black 5s' survive. Running alongside is one of BR's petrol permanent way trolleys, being used by a film crew to record this unique event.

The first of this trio of little tank locomotives is Wantage Tramway 0-4-0 well tank No 5, believed to be the oldest steamable loco in Britain, dating back to 1857. No 5 is now housed at Didcot.

Lancashire & Yorkshire Railway 0-4-0 saddle tank No 51218 was built in 1901, and now works on the Keighley & Worth Valley Railway

This is Class 'A1X' 0-6-0 tank *Fenchurch* from the London, Brighton & South Coast Railway, built in 1872, and now to be found on the Bluebell Railway in Sussex.

Southern Railway Class 'S15' 4-6-0 No 841 was not named while in service but is now called *Greene King* after the brewers. She is one of four survivors from her class.

Also representing the Southern, 'Merchant Navy' Class 4-6-2 No 35028 *Clan Line* carries the headboard of the 'Atlantic Coast Express', a train often hauled by locos of her class, of which 11 survive from a total of 30 built between 1941 and 1949. One of these, No 35011 *General Steam Navigation*, is the only steam loco ever built with the word 'Steam' in its name! She is preserved at the Brighton Railway Museum.

Class 2MT 2-6-2 tank No 41241 was built by BR at Crewe in 1949 to an LMS design, and carries the livery of her home line, the Keighley & Worth Valley Railway. One of 130 built between 1946 and 1952, she is one of only four survivors.

Also BR-built to an LMS design, this time at Darlington in 1951, Class 4MT 2-6-0 No 43106 is the only survivor of her class of 162 built between 1947 and 1952, and now operates on the Severn Valley Railway.

BR Standard Class 4MT 4-6-0 No 75029 was built at Swindon in 1954 and only named *Green Knight* after preservation in 1967. Eighty of this class were built between 1951 and 1957, and six survive.

These BR Standard designs were meant to replace the ageing varieties of locos inherited from the old companies, but were shamefully short-lived, none more so than the final steam locomotive in the Cavalcade, BR 9F 2-10-0 No 92220 *Evening Star*. Built as late as 1960, she was the last of her class of 251, built to haul heavy freight trains, and the last steam locomotive built for British Railways. Eight more of this powerful class still survive.

MID-1970s:
MORE ROUTES OPEN TO STEAM

No 4472 *Flying Scotsman* approaches York from Scarborough, carrying the 'Flying Scotsman' headboard, in June 1976.

The mid-1970s was a time of intense activity in steam railway preservation circles, with further increases in main-line route miles being made available, including York-Carnforth, Guide Bridge-Sheffield, Leeds-York and Skipton-Barrow. The list of locos approved for steam-hauled rail tours was also growing rapidly; examples added included Nos 6201 *Princess Elizabeth*, 1000, the Midland 'Compound', 790 *Hardwicke*, 5900 *Hinderton Hall*, 1306 *Mayflower*, 92220 *Evening Star* and several more Stanier 'Black 5s'.

Apart from the numerous steam charters and all the preparations for the Shildon celebrations, 1975 saw the winding up of the Association of Railway Preservation Society's 'Return to Steam' committee, which had proved so influential in negotiations with BR a few years earlier. In its place was formed the Steam Locomotive Operators Association (SLOA), which would become the champion for main-line steam in the years ahead. The new organisation would soon be called upon in this role as, at the start of 1976, the British Railways Board announced its new policy for the years 1976-79 inclusive, which sent shock-waves through the preservation movement. Its major points were:

* Steam operations were expected to reduce gradually during the period and the situation would be reviewed in 1978, but by the early 1980s it was foreseen that major steam running would no longer be allowed.

* Almost 300 miles of approved steam routes were withdrawn, including Sheffield-York-Newcastle and Oxford-Hereford, although York-Harrogate-Leeds was added, leaving a total of 918 miles.

* Locomotives would be confined to their home areas.

* No steam would be allowed over the Settle-Carlisle route.

* Restrictions concerning the months of the year and days of the week (i.e. Saturday and Sunday only) when steam could run would remain in place.

* All applications to run tours must be made through the SLOA.

All this generated a predictably hostile reception. Could it be that 1980 would see the end of steam on the main line? Was all the optimism and excitement of the early 1970s to be so short-lived?

1970S STEAM SPECIALS

Despite doubts about the future, main-line steam continued to attract the attention of the public as 'steam specials' criss-crossed the country.

On the main line again, 9F No 92220 *Evening Star*, the last steam loco built for BR, heads the 'Pioneer Express' out of York for Scarborough in August 1976.

With the York-Carnforth route now open to steam, the two railway centres are connected directly once more and in October 1976 ex-LNER 'A4' No 4498 *Sir Nigel Gresley* hauls 'The Pennine Venturer' towards Bentham.

In the same month, ex-LNER 'B1' No 1306 *Mayflower*, recently overhauled at Horwich Works in preparation for the Shildon Cavalcade, pilots ex-LMS 'Black 5' No 5407 racing through Bentham station with 'The Pennine Dalesman' rail tour.

Ex-LMS 'Princess Royal' Class No 6201 *Princess Elizabeth* passes Marshbrook Crossing near Church Stretton, heading for Shrewsbury with the 'Mercian Venturer' in October 1976.

'Black 5' No 5305 waits at Carnforth station, having brought the 'Humber Venturer' from Hull during April 1978 on the first leg of its journey to Barrow-in-Furness.

The train crosses Arnside
Viaduct at the northern
end of Morecambe Bay,
with LNER 'B1' No
1306 *Mayflower* now in
charge.

THE LAST YEARS OF THE 1970S

The last years of the 1970s saw great activity in steam circles, in marked
contrast to the mood of despondency that had descended on the main-
line steam movement during the middle years of the decade. 1978 saw a
major turning of the tide in terms of BR policy, maybe the most important
change of heart since steam had returned to the main line in 1971. This was
the announcement by BR that it now intended to market a new programme of

LNER 'V2' No 4771
Green Arrow accelerates
away from York past
Chaloners Whin Junction
during July 1978.

its own steam-hauled trains under the banner 'Full Steam Ahead – for all the family', in addition to the 19 promoted by the SLOA. All these tours proved highly popular and such was the pressure of bookings that additional trains were added to the itinerary. The corner had indeed been turned, and the mood among enthusiasts had changed from despondency to elation in just a couple of years. The threat to end steam running had been withdrawn and the flood-gates looked to be opening, as steam specials were now in abundance with the 'old favourites'

LMS 'Jubilee' Class No 5690 *Leander* approaches York near Copmanthorpe with the 'Mancunian' rail tour from Dinting Railway Centre in October 1978. On the return leg of the tour she is piloted by Midland 'Compound' No 1000 near Bolton Percy.

performing regularly and 'new additions' featuring in the growing contingent of 'must-see' restorations. These included LMS 'Royal Scot' Class No 6115 *Scots Guardsman*, 'K1' No 2005 and the legendary LNER 'A4' *Mallard*. At Bridgnorth No 70000 *Britannia* was at last steamed again in 1978, after a restoration project taking seven years to complete.

On the down side, 1978 saw the sad and untimely death of the Bishop of Wakefield, The Right Reverend Eric Treacy MBE, at Appleby station on the Settle & Carlisle line. There to photograph a steam special hauled by No 92220 *Evening Star*, he stumbled and fell on the bridge and suffered a major heart attack. Held in the highest regard among both railway enthusiasts and photographers, Bishop Treacy would be greatly missed, but will always be remembered for his outstanding railway photography.

1979 saw steam return to Paddington station for its '125' celebrations in the shape of GWR 'King' No 6000 *King George V*, 'Hall' No 5900 *Hinderton Hall* and, later in the year, 'Castle' No 5051 *Drysllwyn Castle* and BR's 9F No 92220 *Evening Star*.

LMS 'Jubilee' No 5690 *Leander* at work near York again, this time racing through Church Fenton in February 1979.

'V2' No 4771 enters York station in April 1979 with the 'Northumbrian Limited'.

LNER 'A3' No 4472 *Flying Scotsman* runs through Marston Moor station en route for York with the 'Yorkshire Circular' tour in August 1979.

SR 'Merchant Navy' Class No 35028 *Clan Line* enters York MPD, also in August 1979.

With the 'Yorkshire Circular' rail tour, 'V2' No 4771 *Green Arrow* heads for York from Harrogate through the country station at Poppleton in August 1979.

Right: LNER 'A4' No 4498 *Sir Nigel Gresley* waits to leave Carnforth station in charge of the newly instigated 'Cumbrian Coast Express' on 21 August 1979.

Below: In celebration of 'Rocket 150', LMS 'Jubilee' No 5690 *Leander* hauls her train along the Liverpool to Manchester main line through Eccles.

INTO THE 1980s

Leander is seen again near Earlstown on 10 August 1980.

The major railway event of 1980 was 'Rocket 150', a celebration at Rainhill to mark 150 years of the Liverpool & Manchester Railway, opened on 15 September 1830. Many steam tours and exhibitions were staged throughout the summer and autumn, concentrated in the North West, with the aim of promoting the cavalcade to re-enact the 'Rainhill Trials'. To be held from the 24 to 26 May, 100,000 grandstand seats were sold to those eager to view this historic event. Special trains hauled by such locos as *Lord Nelson, Duchess of Hamilton* and *Leander* were integral in focussing public awareness on this important landmark in our railway heritage, as BR promoted the tours with the slogan 'Full Steam Ahead – in Rocket 150 Year'.

The Settle-Carlisle route took centre stage from the start. In 1980 the SLOA planned to run six trains advertised as the 'Cumbrian Mountain Express' between Skipton and Carlisle. Such was the demand for seats that a further six were organised, carrying more than 5,000 passengers over the famous line. Steam on the main lines was firmly back in business.

In 1981 more than 100 steam-hauled trains ran on British Rail, of which BR itself had contributed 59. A decade had passed since the first steam returned to the main lines and the preservation movement,

SR No 850 (BR No 30850) *Lord Nelson* brings the 'Scarborough Spa Express' back to York across Bootham Junction level crossing on 12 August 1981.

LNER 'A3' No 4472
Flying Scotsman takes the
'Scarborough Spa Express'
outwards to Scarborough
past Burton Lane, the
junction for the Derwent
Valley line, on 24 August
1981.

with the considerable backing of BR, was going
from strength to strength. Mid-week runs such
as Eastern Region's 'Scarborough Spa Express'
and London Midland Region's 'Cumbrian
Coast Express' were proving increasingly
popular. Together with the regular attraction of
the 'Cumbrian Mountain Express' on Tuesdays,
the early years of the 1980s were proving to be a
high-water point, with many services being over-
subscribed. Motive power for the BR-sponsored
trains was entrusted to such favourites as Nos
4472 *Flying Scotsman*, 4498 *Sir Nigel Gresley*,
46229 *Duchess of Hamilton*, 5690 *Leander*, LMS
'Black 5s' 5305 and 5407, 777 *Sir Lamiel* and
34092 *City of Wells*. Combined with this was the
SLOA's programme, also wonderfully successful,
boasting a load factor approaching 100% in
1982. It came as no surprise, therefore, when it
was announced that steam running on BR main
lines was to be extended to 1990, although the
initial elation was short-lived as 1983 dawned
with the jaw-dropping revelation that BR
intended to close the most popular of all the
routes used for steam excursions – the Settle &
Carlisle line. As well as dismay, the result was a
massive surge in passenger usage over the line, with steam charters hugely over-
subscribed and ordinary service trains having to be increased from the normal
four coaches to ten to cope with the demand for seats.

As the 1980s progressed, the success story of steam running continued,
with further famous locos showing off their pulling power. Nos 92220 *Evening
Star*, 4771 *Green Arrow*, 60009 *Union of South Africa*, 3440 *City of Truro*, 4930
Hagley Hall and 7029 *Clun Castle* were among those making regular and popular
appearances. The SLOA had taken over responsibility for the 'Cumbrian
Mountain Express' and the 'Cumbrian Coast Express' from BR, and these,
together with the extended 'Scarborough Spa Express' still run by the Eastern
Region, continued to draw the crowds. All this provided added incentive to the
preservation groups to renovate their locos to the highest standards in order for
them to be accepted into the SLOA's now official operating list.

Completing a trilogy
of famous names, LMS
'Duchess' No 46229
Duchess of Hamilton
heads for the coast on 16
August 1983.

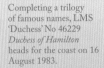

LMS 'Jubilee' No
5690 *Leander* pauses
at Bingley on 12 April
1982 with the Leeds-
Carnforth 'Trans
Pennine Pullman', over
another route opened to
steam in the mid-1970s.

IS STEAM PRESERVATION UNSTOPPABLE?

By the time the 1980s were under way the steam railway preservation movement seemed unstoppable. All over the country, preserved lines were attracting growing numbers of 'closet enthusiasts' keen to relive steam experiences of yesteryear for themselves and their young families. Existing societies were extending operations, and new ones were breathing life back into lines once given up for dead. 1968 was long enough ago for the nostalgia to kick in, yet recent enough to remain fresh in the memory.

By 1985 180 steam excursions were booked to run on BR lines, and a gradual feeling of 'overkill' was beginning to pervade the steam scene, as the long period of passenger increases showed the inevitable signs of having peaked. BR and the SLOA were forced to rethink their programmes and, after much hard-headed discussions, a more cost-effective programme was agreed with the result that what might have developed into a financial crisis was rescued. Passenger numbers were still disappointing when compared to recent 'highs' but, with the return of No 4468 *Mallard* to the main line after a £35,000 overhaul at the National Railway Museum in York, spirits were lifted and passenger numbers rallied once more. For SLOA Marketing though, this proved to be the end of the line, as its failure to adequately promote its programme of steam-hauled enthusiasts' trains led to its withdrawal from future participation from 1987. The result was a new policy from BR of 'franchising' steam-hauled tours, with a variety of operators becoming involved, including individual former members of the SLOA. This was to prove highly successful as more steam specials were sponsored under the new arrangements and further 'favourites' welcomed back into the growing list of 'regulars' in charge of trains. These included Nos 6201 *Princess Elizabeth* and 6000 *King George V*.

Most momentous of all, on 9 March 1989 the Minister for Public Transport,

A most welcome return to main-line steam working was LNER 'A4' No 4468 *Mallard*, seen here flying through Bentham, between Carnforth and Settle Junction, with, appropriately, the 'Birdwatch Europe Express' on 16 May 1987.

Michael Portillo MP, finally announced to the House of Commons that, because of the weight of new evidence, there would be a 'stay of execution' for the legendary Settle & Carlisle line until mid-October, reversing previous policy in a gigantic U-turn and promoting it now as a 'BR Leisure Line', together with the Cumbrian Coast route, the Tyne Valley line, the Esk Valley line and the Blackburn to Hellifield line.

Mr Portillo also announced that he was still considering proposals from private bidders hopeful of taking over the line, and soon afterwards an all-party 'Settle and Carlisle Group' was set up to keep the Minister informed of the strength of public opinion supporting the saving of the line. Their efforts, together with those from Flying Scotsman Services, which organised and ran a further ten 'Cumbrian Mountain Express' tours over the line during the summer, finally led to the announcement, to the delight of railway enthusiasts nationwide, that he had refused to allow BR to close either the Settle & Carlisle or the connecting Blackburn to Hellifield line. Throughout the 1980s steam specials had continued to draw the crowds, and when BR finally abandoned its thoroughly misguided policy of refusing to release their timings, we were all, at last, able to enjoy the steam revival. How times have moved on and attitudes changed since the initial 'five routes' were grudgingly released to the steam community in 1972!

The York-Scarborough line was one of the 'five routes' opened to steam in 1972. Now part of the 'Scarborough Spa Express' tour, which sees the locos giving good value as they take the 'special' on a 12-hour journey from York, through Knaresborough and Harrogate to Leeds, back through York to Scarborough for the afternoon at the coast, then back through York to Leeds, Harrogate and Knaresborough and finally back to York.

TOWARDS THE 1990S

Thus the unstoppable railway preservation movement steamed on through the late 1980s and into the 1990s, 20 years and more, with every year bringing its own memorable events.

In 1986 the unique BR 'Pacific' No 71000 *Duke of Gloucester* completed its trial run on the Great Central Railway on 25 May, after a long restoration project. On 9 July of that year 'A4' 'Pacific' No 4468 *Mallard* returned to the main line by heading the first 'Scarborough Spa Express' of the season.

In 1987, as well as the opening of the East Lancashire Railway, the Embsay & Bolton Abbey Railway extended its line to Holywell, while steam returned to the Cambrian in Wales with ex-GWR No 7819 *Hinton Manor* and BR Standard 4MT No 75069 in steam.

The rush to buy locos from Woodham's scrapyard at Barry Dock had gathered pace as cutting-up had recommenced in 1981, but by 1988 the famous 'graveyard' had given up its last loco, GWR '2800' Class 2-8-0 No 2873, the 213th to be so rescued from the site.

1988 also saw steam return to the recently reopened Birmingham Snow Hill station, with GWR No 7029 *Clun Castle* in charge of a train carrying HRH The Prince of Wales on a visit to the Birmingham Railway Museum at Tyseley.

In 1989 the Settle & Carlisle route was back in business after its reprieve, with regular steam specials gracing this magnificent railway line, while on the North Wales Coast route steam trains were running again to Llandudno and Holyhead from Crewe, hauled by Bulleid 'Pacific' Nos 35028 *Clan Line* and 34027 *Taw Valley*, LMS No 6201 *Princess Elizabeth* or 'Black 5' No 5407. Also

For many, the sight of steam tackling the mighty Settle & Carlisle line, itself threatened with closure for so long, represents all that the preservation movement has battled so hard to achieve. In November 1983 LMS 'Duchess' No 46229 *Duchess of Hamilton* reaches Ais Gill, the summit of the 'Long Drag', with the 'Cumbrian Mountain Pullman'. Two success stories rolled into one!

Beautifully preserved and restored to full main-line running order, Gresley 'A4' 'Pacific' No 4498 *Sir Nigel Gresley* heads a Bradford to Carlisle enthusiasts' special at Appleby, on the iconic Settle & Carlisle line, during September 1993.

welcomed back to the main line that year was LMS 'Jubilee' No 45596 *Bahamas*.

However, the concern that had been expressed on a recurring basis throughout the late 1980s, that there was a danger of too many steam tours chasing too few passengers at a time of a worsening economic climate and rising interest rates, finally came to a head in 1990, when decisions were reluctantly taken to reduce the number of excursions, to run only one steam special on any day and to use a limited number of well-proven routes with large engines pulling heavy trains.

This worked well, undoubtedly helped by the return of No 4472 *Flying Scotsman* to main-line service following its 'holiday' in Australia, No 46229 back in service after overhaul, and BR Standard Class 8 'Pacific' No 71000 *Duke of Gloucester* taking trains between Marylebone and Nottingham and later over the Settle & Carlisle route. 1990 also was the year that LMS 'Princess Royal' No 46203 *Princess Margaret Rose* returned to steam on the Derby to Sheffield line after 28 years out of service, while on the Bluebell Railway 9F 2-10-0 No 92240 was welcomed back into steam after a 12-year restoration programme.

In 1991 LNER 'A2' No 60532 *Blue Peter* returned to steam on the North Yorkshire Moors Railway, while BR 'Pacific' No 70000 *Britannia* was steamed at Carnforth for the first time in four years and, together with LNER 'A3' No 4472 *Flying Scotsman*, was soon taking steam specials from Cambridge to Kings Lynn. The omens seemed set for a glorious decade to come.

1992 saw *Blue Peter* and *Duke of Gloucester* on main-line duty again, while in Scotland ex-NBR 'K' Class No 256 *Glen Douglas* left Glasgow Transport Museum after 26 years, to return to Bo'ness with the intention of making her available to run on the West Highland Line. At home in York, the National Railway Museum reopened after a refurbishment costing £6 million and, although the recession was biting deeply, the movement as a whole was in good shape and the future prospects looked bright indeed.

By the end of 1992 approximately 550 former BR locomotives had been or were in the process of being preserved and restored. This number does not include the great many 'industrial' locos that had not been in the ownership of BR or had not operated under the jurisdiction of the British Railways Board or its constituents. Nor does this number include narrow-gauge or foreign-built locos, several of which have been imported to work on our preserved lines. It does include, however, War Department locos and those operated by the US Army Transportation Corps.

Of this 550 or so locomotives, their sources and approximate numbers are as follows. The GWR contributed the most (160), followed by the LMS (130), then the SR (90), the War Department (80), the LNER (50), and BR itself (50). The classes with the most survivors are the LMS 5MT 4-6-0s – the 'Black 5s' – with 18 still going strong, followed by BR's 4MT 2-6-4Ts, with 15. Among the major classes of passenger and heavy freight locos to be saved, from the GWR we have 11 of its 4-6-0 'Hall' design, followed by the 4-6-0 'Manor' class (nine preserved), 4-6-0 'Castles' (eight), 4-6-0 'Modified Halls' (seven) and 4-6-0 'Kings' (three).

From the LMS, four 6P5F 'Jubilee' Class 4-6-0s survive, together with 7P 'Royal Scot' Class 4-6-0s (three), 8P 'Coronation' Class 4-6-2s (three), 7P 'Princess Royal' 4-6-2s (two) and, from the heavy freight stock, eight 8F 2-8-0s.

LNER survivors include six from the 'A4' 4-6-2 class, two 'B1' 4-6-0s, one 'A2' 4-6-2 (*Blue Peter*), one 'A3' 4-6-2 (*Flying Scotsman*), one 'V2' 2-6-2 (*Green Arrow*), and one 'K1', No 62005.

From the SR there are 11 surviving 'Merchant Navy' Class 4-6-2s, 10 from the 'West Country/Battle of Britain' Class of 4-6-2s, and a further 10 'Rebuilt BB/WC' Class. There are also five Maunsell 'S15' 4-6-0s, three 'Schools' Class 4-4-0s, one 'N15' 'King Arthur' Class (No 30777 *Sir Lamiel*), and one 'Lord Nelson' 4-6-0 (*Lord Nelson* itself).

Ex-BR loco designs remaining include nine of the 9F 2-10-0 heavy freight locomotives, two 7P6F 'Britannia' Class 4-6-2s, ten 4MT 4-6-0s, five 5MT 4-6-0s and of course the single 8P 4-6-2 loco to be built, No 71000 *Duke of Gloucester*.

An early inspiration, and probably the first 'new-build', to use the now popular description, was the working replica of George Stephenson's *Locomotion*, built for the Stockton & Darlington 150th anniversary celebrations of 1975, and later housed at Beamish Open Air Museum, followed in 1979 by another, this time of his famous *Rocket*, which had taken part in the Rainhill Trials. It was fitting, therefore, that this replica should be at the forefront of the British Rail celebrations commemorating the 150th anniversary of the Liverpool and Manchester Railway in 1980. She is seen here

working at the National Railway Museum, York, in 2001, with the author on the footplate and again *(above)* in February 2010. *Author/ Frances Townsend*

'New-build' Peppercorn
'A1' No 60163 *Tornado*,
as yet without nameplate,
approaches York near
Shipton with the
'Talisman', a Darlington-
King's Cross tour, on 2
February 2009.

New Century, New Builds

Looking back over the years to those first faltering steps on the bumpy road of steam preservation, what has been achieved is little short of miraculous. 'Steam is finished on our railways' was the official verdict delivered in 1968. What a debt we owe to those who refused to accept the death sentence handed down to our fleet of outmoded and thereby condemned steam locomotives.

Even that stalwart and legendary railway photographer, Bishop Eric Treacy MBE, could not have foreseen the rise of the steam preservation movement. In an article for *The Railway Magazine* published in December 1967 entitled 'Reflections of a Railway Photographer', he had this to say on the subject of the future of railway photography: 'I do not see much future in the hobby.' He went on to predict that '…within about five years we shall see a considerable diminution in the activities of railway photographers. They will be concentrating on a rapidly diminishing number of relics of the steam age.'

He would no doubt be astounded and delighted to know that the art is not dead, that at linesides up and down the country enthusiasts young and old still flock to capture the fleeting moment of the passing steam train. Rather than rapidly diminishing, steam stock continues to increase.

GWR 'Castle' No 5043
Earl of Mount Edgcumbe
passes Colton with the
return 'City of York'
Tyseley-York tour of 19
April 2009.

On an extremely cold and wet day at Blea Moor, with the landscape all but lost in the mist, 'K1' No 62005 *Lord of the Isles* makes 'heavy weather' of the climb over the Settle & Carlisle line on 4 May 2009 with the 'North Eastern Mountaineer'.

From a slow, often faltering beginning, the tide gradually turned and gained an unstoppable momentum, until the whole country seemed to be in the grip of the steam nostalgia movement. Where are we now in terms of the steam scene, and where do we go from here?

2009 was a momentous year for the steam locomotive. The season got off to a flying start with the West Somerset Railway's Spring Gala. Although its claim to be Britain's longest heritage line, at 24 miles, had recently been eclipsed by the newly opened (narrow-gauge) Welsh Highland Railway, at 27 miles (and which, linked with the Ffestiniog Railway, now boasted a 40-mile steam railway journey), the West Somerset pulled out all the stops to stage a 'standard gauge spectacular' by gathering an impressive collection of locos representing the 'Big Four' companies. Those on duty during the event included LMS 'Royal Scot' 4-6-0 No 6100 *Royal Scot*, 'Black 5' No 45231 *The Sherwood Forester*, and SR 'Rebuilt West Country' Class 'Pacifics' Nos 34028 *Eddystone* and 34046 *Braunton*. From the LNER there was 'A4' 'Pacific' No 60019 *Bittern*, and from the GWR came 4-6-0 No 4936 *Kinlet Hall*.

'New-build' 'A1' 'Pacific' No 60163 *Tornado* was scheduled for a busy time during 2009, with a series of testing runs including the still daunting Settle & Carlisle line.

Much more pleasant conditions welcomed the Hellifield to Carlisle 'Settle-Carlisle Express' on 17 May, with 'Jubilee' No 5690 *Leander* in charge.

Next day, 18 May 2009, saw LNER 'A4' No 60009 *Union of South Africa* heading for York near Shipton-by-Beningborough with Day 3 of the 'Coronation' tour, the Edinburgh-York leg.

April and May saw a full calendar on the main line, with no fewer than 35 steam-hauled excursions involving tours to all corners of the UK. Among the locos taking charge were LMS 'Duchess' No 6233 *Duchess of Sutherland*, 'Princess Royal' No 6201 *Princess Elizabeth*, 'Jubilee' No 5690 *Leander*, 'Britannia' No 70013 *Oliver Cromwell*, 'Royal Scot' No 46115 *Scots Guardsman* and 'Black 5' No 45407 *The Lancashire Fusilier*. As well as *Tornado*, the LNER was represented by 'A4' Nos 60007 *Sir Nigel Gresley* and 60009 *Union of South Africa*, together with 'K1' No 62005 *Lord of the Isles*. The SR locos Nos 35028 *Clan Line* and 34067 *Tangmere* were busy, and for the GWR Nos 6024 *King Edward I* and 5043 *Earl of Mount Edgcumbe* saw regular service.

Thus the scene was set, and as spring turned into summer *Tornado* was fully booked, doing a round of the preserved lines as well as her main-line commitments, and every weekend saw several steam-hauled 'specials' gracing tracks up and down the country, supplemented by mid-week 'extras' now that the weather was improving. Added to this impressive itinerary, every preserved line seemed to be holding its own 'galas', attracting visitors by the thousand.

By July *Tornado* had clocked up an impressive 10,000 miles in main-line service, and everywhere she travelled crowds packed the lineside to glimpse this now world-famous loco. Throughout the country, the steam revolution was attracting vast numbers of all ages and the preservation societies were at full stretch, so much so that one, the North Yorkshire Moors Railway – Britain's most popular heritage line – had to cancel some steam trains during August due to a shortage of drivers.

The 'new build' phenomenon was set to escalate on the back of the runaway success of *Tornado*, with the Great Western Society's plan to recreate an example of Churchward's 'Saint' Class 4-6-0s in the form of No 2999 *Lady of Legend*, 'back-converted' from 'Hall' No 4942 *Maindy Hall*.

Summer turned to autumn and the passion for steam among the general public showed no sign of abating. 'Autumn Steam Galas' attracted hordes to every preserved line and main-line steam seemed to fill every available slot. Such a demanding itinerary inevitably has its costs, and major overhauls and restorations are a fact of life, with recent 'losses' from the steam fleet including LMS No 6100 *Royal Scot* and the iconic 'Duchess' No 46229 *Duchess of Hamilton*, both requiring major and extremely expensive restoration work if they are to be seen again in all their glory in the near future.

Perhaps the most significant project to gain momentum as 2009 drew towards winter was the plan to build a new Fowler 'Patriot' Class locomotive. To be named *The Unknown Warrior* and carrying the number 45551, this 'new-build' has been designated as the National Memorial Engine, to be a 'living tribute' to all the British and Commonwealth servicemen and women who gave so much in the two World Wars and numerous other conflicts in order to help make our world a better place. It is planned that the new loco should be ready in time for the centenary of the First World War Armistice in 2018.

As winter 2009 approached, the 'Second Steam Age' was well established. There had been more than 400 main-line steam charters during the year, hauled by 27 different locomotives. In the five months from the middle of May, only on eight of the 148 days was no steam haulage seen on our main lines, and the period 4 July to 11 October saw 93 consecutive days where steam was running somewhere on the network, with Sunday 23 August claiming the record with no fewer than seven steam charters during a week in which 26 steam tours ran.

Alas it was not all good news. For all the successes of our growing steam fleet, there were also the losses – locos that had graced our nation's tracks in the 40 years or so since 1968, but for which, in the majority of cases, there seems little prospect of a come-back. These include such famous names as Nos 6998 *Burton Agnes Hall*, 6000 *King George V* and 7029 *Clun Castle* from the GWR, 34016 *Bodmin* and 34092 *City of Wells* from the Southern, 4468 *Mallard*, 60800 *Green Arrow* and 60592 *Blue Peter* from the LNER, and from the LMS 45596 *Bahamas*, 46203 *Princess Margaret Rose* and 46229 *Duchess of Hamilton*, not forgetting ex-LNWR No 790 *Hardwicke*, ex-Midland 'Compound' No 1000 and of course BR's legendary 'last steam loco', 9F 2-10-0 No 92220 *Evening Star*.

Perhaps the massive success that made 2009 the pinnacle of the steam revival in the UK so far will continue despite the recession, and maybe funding will be found to restore these and other much-loved locos, to once again take their place at the head of steam specials in the years to come. If the published plans for special events, galas and steam tours are anything to go by, the future looks rosy indeed!

What an incredible journey! How could any of us have imagined, back in the dark days following 1968, that within two decades steam locomotives would move from pariahs to prodigals, from dirty and outdated relics of the Industrial Revolution to classic powerhouses of engineering, essential in the education of our children, to be welcomed back with open arms into the national railway family?

No longer the realm of the small boy in short trousers, or the 'anorak' with no friends and no life, the rehabilitation of the steam locomotive has become an issue of national pride. More and more of us are taking time to seek out and enjoy the resurgence of this phenomenon, as the steam railway preservation movement grows from strength to ever increasing strength, with record numbers of visitors, young and old, flocking to the preserved lines, and 'steam specials' up and down the country full to capacity every week.

That which was condemned as an unacceptable drain on resources has become a major source of profit. How times do change!

The 'Scarborough Spa Express' is always good value, and here 'Britannia' No 70013 *Oliver Cromwell* takes the train away from Poppleton towards Harrogate on 27 August 2009.

On 13 December 2009, at Goose Hill Junction between Wakefield and Normanton, LMS 'Princess Royal' Class No 6201 *Princess Elizabeth* storms the bank with the Liverpool-York 'York Yule-tide Express'.

Snow covers the Yorkshire landscape north of York as LNER 'A4' No 60007 *Sir Nigel Gresley* races past Shipton-by-Beningborough with the King's Cross-Newcastle 'Christmas Tynesider' tour on 19 December 2009.

This was to be the beginning of a new era for me in 1972. Steam preservation was fast becoming big business as the potential attraction of the nostalgia movement was quickly being realised on a countrywide scale. At that time steam was still almost totally confined to privately owned 'light railways' (preserved

'Jubilee' No 5690 *Leander* draws the crowds during her visit to the Birmingham Railway Museum at Tyseley in 1972, home of the Standard Gauge Steam Trust – although it seems that not every visitor was enthralled!

A little 'TLC' for her nameplate.

lines) or the 'live museums' such as Carnforth, Didcot, Tyseley and Dinting Railway Centre, where in April 1969 15,000 steam enthusiasts had visited a 'Steam Weekend' that featured LMS 'Jubilee' No 5596 *Bahamas* on its first public steaming since preservation. Other locos on display during 1972 included L&YR 2-4-2T No 1008, built at Horwich in 1899, LSWR 4-4-0 No 120 from the same year, SR 4-6-0 No 770 *Sir Lamiel* and SR 4-4-0 No 925 *Cheltenham*, all transferred from the BR National Relics Store, Brighton, on long-term loan. These had been added to the Trust's growing stock, which also included LMS 'Black 5' No 5428 *Eric Treacy* and GWR Hall No 4983 *Albert Hall*.

Tyseley MPD was a comparatively recent steam shed. The station there was not built until 1906, and on completion in 1908 the shed consisted of two roundhouses – one for passenger engines and the other for freight – a small workshop and a coaling stage. Rationalisation following the take-over of control of the Western Region's West Midlands territory by the London Midland Region in 1963 led to the shed's

Undergoing restoration at Tyseley at the same time as the visit of *Leander*, LMS 'Princess Royal' Class No 6201 *Princess Elizabeth* is under wraps.

freight roundhouse being demolished in that year, with the workshop following in 1964 and the closure of the steam depot in 1967, accompanied by the further demolition of the passenger roundhouse.

On 6 June 1968 restored LMS 'Jubilee' 4-6-0 No 5593 was renamed *Kolhapur* during a ceremony outside the former coaling stage led by Sir Eric Clayson, Chairman of the Birmingham Post & Mail Limited. This represented the culmination of many thousands of hours of work by members of 7029 Clun Castle Limited, supported by professional railwaymen from BR. The company

hoped to house No 5593 and its other preserved locomotive, GWR 'Castle' No 7029 *Clun Castle* at the site, which had been converted into an engine shed by the addition of an extension with smoke extractors in the roof. Dubbed 'Birmingham's Most Modern Steam Shed' in a *Railway Magazine* article at the time, the building 'has been cleaned out, redecorated, had electrical wiring renewed and fluorescent lighting and 13-amp power points fitted.' An additional facility was provided by the acquisition of a former BR Bogie Engineers' Saloon, No M45021M, 'for use as a "club-room" in which members of its works team can relax'. 7029 Clun Castle Limited thus now felt able to invite visits from organised parties of railway enthusiasts to its facilities, for which a 'nominal charge' would be made.

In 1969 the Standard Gauge Steam Trust was founded with the intention of creating a locomotive workshop to form the basis of an industrial museum on the Tyseley site, leased from BR. Work soon started on a wheel-drop pit and new workshops, and when regular steam 'Open Days' and later steam excursions met with increasing public support, the future was starting to look increasingly bright.

The Standard Gauge Steam Trust's site at Tyseley is composed of the former GWR depot together with its associated coaling facilities and workshops, which themselves have undergone restoration in order to be capable of providing an essential maintenance facility for steam locomotives, including a wheel tyre and crankpin turning lathe in addition to an electric wheel-drop. It also serves as a base for authorised steam running over BR tracks. The Trust's collection was begun in 1966 with *Clun Castle*, quickly followed by the 'Jubilee' *Kolhapur*. Having both seen extensive service including use on steam specials in the last years of steam on BR, they were further evidence of the need for repair and restoration provision, including to the privately owned railways, which themselves for the most part could carry out only minor repairs.

By the early 1980s the Birmingham Railway Museum Steam Depot, as it had become known, had become a centre for 'Steam on BR' rail tours over BR lines to Stratford-upon-Avon and Didcot via Oxford. The Vintage Trains Society, formerly known as The Friends of Birmingham Railway Museum, exists to promote the projects operated by the Trust, which now include the 'Vintage Trains' main-line operation and the 'Shakespeare Express' rail tours. Vintage Trains operates trains on the main line using locos from the Tyseley collection, with excursions to places of interest such as Edinburgh and featuring routes such as the iconic Settle & Carlisle line. The 'Shakespeare Express' is the Vintage Trains regular summer steam run between Birmingham and Stratford-upon-Avon, which operates on Sundays between July and mid-September, involving 50 miles of main-line steam travel.

Locomotive stock has increased to include GWR 'Castle' Nos 5043 *Earl of Mount Edgcumbe*, 5080 *Defiant* and 7027 *Thornbury Castle*, as well as several other locos of GWR origin, together with coaching stock that features Pullman cars, a Gresley buffet car and two 'semi Royal Saloons'. Plans are also afoot for the construction of a roundhouse small exhibits museum, station and other ancillary features.

The operation continues to prosper and develop into a major steam centre, whose engineering subsidiary, Tyseley Locomotive Works, has a well-earned reputation for the restoration, maintenance and servicing of steam, classic diesel and electric locomotives, as well as coaches to main-line standards.

Recent open days have proved especially popular, with thousands of visitors attending the events, and more are planned in the near future. Emphasis at Tyseley now is on running a professional locomotive overhaul and maintenance site, so much so that its facilities are in constant demand from other preserved railways and private operations.

Bluebell Railway

The railway line from Lewes to East Grinstead in Sussex, part of the old London, Brighton & South Coast Railway, was closed by BR in 1958, and the following year saw the birth of the Lewes & East Grinstead Railway Preservation Society. By the end of 1959 a Light Railway Order had been granted by the Ministry of Transport for the line from Sheffield Park to Horsted Keynes, to be known as the Lewes & East Grinstead Railway. The line was re-opened on 7 August 1960 as the 'Bluebell Railway', making it the first preserved standard-gauge steam-operated passenger railway in the world.

Being a former LB&SCR line, the intention was to concentrate on rescuing as much 'Brighton' stock as possible, and luckily BR just happened to have a surplus Stroudley 'Terrier' 0-6-0T for sale. Probably the best-loved of the 'Brighton' designs, the purchase of BR No 32655 and a couple of coaches for £750 was a real bargain. Though the end of steam services on BR was still eight years in the future, the society was soon busy preserving a number of locos and was

At Easter 1987 SR 'Schools' Class No 928 *Stowe* has been dusted down and is being prepared for the summer services.

well on its way to accumulating one of the largest collections of preserved steam locomotives, carriages and wagons in Britain, and to becoming one of the largest tourist attractions in Sussex. However, in that first short summer the Bluebell operated with just four items of stock, each of which hailed from a different company. To supplement the charismatic 'Terrier', ex-South Eastern & Chatham Wainwright 'P' Class 0-6-0T No 31323 (later to be painted blue, renumbered 323 and named *Bluebell*) had been acquired to haul the trains, consisting of a coach from each of the London & South Western Railway and the Southern Railway – not quite the 'all Brighton' ideal with which the railway had been launched. Nevertheless, between commencement on 7 August and the end of the season in October, running only at weekends, visitor numbers exceeded all expectations, and the Bluebell's aim of a volunteer-run steam railway was beginning to prove viable.

The 1960s were not without troubles for the new railway. First, its attempts to acquire the original 'Terrier', No 32636 *Fenchurch* of 1872 vintage, seemed doomed to failure, when a less than sympathetic BR gave the Bluebell just four weeks to complete the deal. It was only after a personal intervention by that notorious East Grinstead resident, Dr Richard Beeching, author of the infamous report *The Reshaping of British Railways*, that the loco was reserved for six months, allowing time for the acquisition to be completed.

In the same year, although the Bluebell had been granted permission to work into Horsted Keynes, which at the time was still used by BR for its electric services to Seaford, a hostile BR management decreed that the railway must purchase the line or close down their operations. Finally, after protracted and desperate negotiations, a hire-purchase deal was struck in 1968 and the Bluebell's days did not come to an untimely end, although, with the termination of BR's involvement at Horsted Keynes, the Bluebell was cut off from the national railway network.

By the early 1970s locomotive stock included BR 4MT 4-6-0 No 75027, GWR 4-4-0 No 3217 *Earl of Berkeley*, LSWR '0415' Class 4-4-2T No 488, dating back to 1885, and a collection of tank locos originating from the LB&SCR and the SE&CR, together with an impressive collection of coaching stock to match. No 488, an Adams Radial Tank loco, had been delivered to the Bluebell Railway as early as June 1961, but was found to be in need of a complete repair, work that

Maunsell-designed 'Q' Class 4F 0-6-0 No 541, introduced in 1938 for the Southern Railway, was also in steam and hauling trains between Sheffield Park and Horsted Keynes, while work was under way to prepare other locos, signal boxes and platforms in preparation for the commencement of the new timetable.

was so beyond the capacity of the Sheffield Park team that it had to be entrusted to BR Engineering at Swindon and, for boiler repairs, BREL at Crewe. She was finally returned to service on 4 August 1973 after repainting in Drummond green by Bluebell Railway staff, the colour to complement her Drummond chimney. Built in Glasgow by Neilson & Co in 1885, she was sold to the Government during the First World War, then went to the East Kent Railway. Later bought by the Southern Railway to work on the Lyme Regis branch, she became No 3488 and, later still, after nationalisation, No 30583, in which guise she became familiar to many enthusiasts in the West Country in the years up to her withdrawal in 1960.

The Bluebell Railway's tracks, straddling the border between East and West Sussex, quickly proved a wise purchase for preservation, with few engineering or operational difficulties to be wrestled with in recreating a railway in the style and character of Victorian England. Running through the low undulating hills, pastures and little woods of the Sussex Weald, the location of the stations at

SR No 541 (BR number 30541) has just arrived from Horsted Keynes and the crew are reversing so she can run round her train ready for the return journey.

At Sheffield Park the platform furniture and fittings have been refreshed and made ready.

each end of the line typify the branch lines that served these parts. At one end of the line, Horsted Keynes station lies in woods a good mile from the village from which it takes its name, while at the other end Sheffield Park station, headquarters of the railway's Locomotive Department, is near no village at all! Having said that, the stations are easily accessible and convenient for visitors, so the new venture flourished. The Southern Victorian atmosphere on the railway is enhanced by staff wearing contemporary uniforms, Victorian costumes are often to be seen, and stations are adorned with colourful enamel advertising signs.

Until 1971, BR 4MT No 75027 was the largest loco operating on the Bluebell line. Then, SR 'West Country' Class 4-6-2 No 34023 *Blackmore Vale* arrived. Preserved by the Bulleid Pacific Preservation Society, she was moved here from the Longmoor Military Railway, when the society's attempt to set up a steam railway failed.

By 1976 major plans were afoot to extend the railway northwards through West Hoathly (site of the original Bluebell Inn), Kingscote and finally to East Grinstead, there to re-establish connection with British Rail. However, this long-term goal of a 'Northern Extension' brought with it another requirement – larger locomotives. In 1976, almost alone among major preservation societies, the Bluebell had no ex-Barry locomotives, but with more pulling power needed from somewhere if the dream was to become a reality, this issue had to be addressed. Over the next two or three years the railway undertook what is believed to be the biggest and costliest road movement of locomotives in the history of railway preservation. From the Barry graveyard came 'S15' 4-6-0 No 30847, 9F 2-10-0 No 92240 and Class 4MT 2-6-4T No 80100, and from Ashchurch came 'Q' 0-6-0 No 30541. All that was needed now was a mammoth fund-raising project to pay for their restoration.

By 1977 a 'Long Term Planning Committee' had been formed to advise on future developments for the railway. These included the restoration of Horsted Keynes to early Southern Railway condition and the redesignation of Sheffield Park, as far as possible, as an LB&SCR area, or at least restored 'in the Brighton style'. Also in the plans are new toilets and a buffet at Sheffield Park, a permanent way depot, extension to the carriage shed, a new museum, the re-siting of Sheffield Park signal box and of course, biggest of them all, extending the line northwards to East Grinstead.

The summer of 1980 would be celebrated in grand style in this part of the railway world, for it marked the 20th anniversary of the opening to the public of the Bluebell Railway, as well as the 150th anniversary of steam railways in the South of England, the Canterbury & Whitstable Railway having opened in May 1830. A major series of events commemorated these landmarks.

The interior of the signal box has been polished to perfection.

In the sheds, Bulleid 'West Country' 'Pacific' No 34023 *Blackmore Vale* is still partially under wraps but is clearly receiving attention to make her ready to renew her role as one of the Bluebell Railway's star performers in the months to come.

By the early 1980s the Bluebell's stock list had swelled to more than 20 locomotives, together with a handful of 'industrials', a substantial collection of pre-nationalisation coaches including SE&CR, Bulleid, Maunsell and Chesham vehicles, and significant freight stock, and though much of this is not Bluebell-owned, it is on loan here because the owners appreciate the facilities available for its care and maintenance.

Meanwhile, progress on the 'Northern Extension' was slow, hampered by opposition from certain landowners, together with the usual and expected obstacles of a physical, technical and financial nature. In other areas, however,

progress had been impressive, with locomotive restoration in the well-equipped repair shop going on apace, and the four-road carriage shed and mechanical area seeing restoration and virtual rebuilding work of the highest order.

Eventually in 1985 planning permission was granted by the Secretaries of State for the Environment and for Transport for the extension to East Grinstead, and the appropriate Light Railway Order was obtained. At last the remaining land could be purchased, and work could begin on track-laying, repairs to Imberhorne Viaduct and the construction of a new Bluebell Railway station at East Grinstead. Work is progressing steadily, though the one remaining obstacle is literally just that – Imberhorne Tip – a massive domestic refuse site from the 1960s and '70s, the contents of which will now have to be removed trainload by trainload in order finally to be able to lay the last section of track, which will restore the Bluebell's direct access to the national network and connect once more with the outside world.

At Horsted Keynes, 'Q' No 541 takes a breather before tackling the run back to Sheffield Park.

The project, known as 'Waste by Rail', continued apace, using GBRf trains during 2011. The operation is now in its fifth (and final?) phase before the 'deadline' imposed by the introduction of the 'Landfill Tax', which comes into force on 1 April 2012, renders the work too expensive to continue.

The pioneer preserved standard-gauge passenger-carrying railway's motto, 'Floreat Vapor' – 'May Steam Flourish', – remains as apposite as ever.

Bodmin & Wenford Railway

The Bodmin branch line was built by the Great Western Railway and opened in 1887 from Bodmin Road, on the Cornwall Railway's 'broad gauge' line from Plymouth to Falmouth, to Bodmin General, the terminus of the GWR's Bodmin branch. Bodmin General was originally named simply 'Bodmin', but later qualified to distinguish it from the other stations of Bodmin North and Bodmin Road. It had a single-sided platform with two adjacent lines, one used as a run-round, two sidings, signal box, goods shed and engine shed. The engine shed closed in April 1962 and passenger services ended on 30 January 1967, with freight services being run down from 1 May of that year, followed inevitably by the closure of the signal box.

Above: The welcoming entrance to the Bodmin and Wenford Railway at the town's General station. *Peter Townsend*

By 1975 two freight services were scheduled daily from Bodmin Road: a Class 25-hauled train to Wadebridge and back, and a Class 08 shunter-hauled train to Wenford Bridge china clay works, though the running of both depended entirely on whether there was traffic to be moved on that particular day. The line to the china clay works crossed remote country roads by ungated level crossings, the end of the line being half a mile short of the original terminus at Wenford

Left: Both surviving '0298' Class 2-4-0WT Beattie 'well tanks' Nos 30585 and 30587 of 1874, that once worked the mineral branch from Boscarne Junction to Wenford Bridge are reunited at Bodmin General during the 2010 Autumn Gala. GWR '5700' Class 0-6-0PT No 4612 is also present. *Peter Townsend*

A further view featuring the Beattie 'well tanks', looking down the line towards Bodmin Parkway from the signal box steps. *Peter Townsend*

Bridge itself – the furthest point from Waterloo on the LSWR line.

The line closed officially on 3 October 1983 with the ending of the freight traffic in and out of English China Clay's Wenford operation, when an 08 shunter brought the last load of clay from the dries and the line fell silent, for a time…

The Bodmin Railway Preservation Society was formed in 1984 and held its first 'Open Day' at Bodmin General two years later. A Light Railway Order was granted in 1989, which allowed the operation of passenger trains over the 3½ miles to Bodmin Road station (now named Bodmin Parkway), with its interchange with the national network. A 1996 extension to a new station at Boscarne Junction gave a total of 6½ miles of track. Latterly the Bodmin & Wenford has acquired an impressive stock of steam, diesel and industrial locomotives. GWR locos include Churchward '4200' Class 2-8-0T No 4247, introduced in 1910, Collett '5700' Class 0-6-0PT No 4612 of 1933, Churchward '4575' Class 2-6-2T No 5552 of 1927, and Collett '6400' Class 0-6-0PT No 6435 of 1932. Former LSWR locos include Drummond 'T9' Class 4-4-0 No 30120 of 1899, part of the National Collection, and '0298' Class 2-4-0WT No 30587 of 1874, a Beattie 'well tank' that once worked the mineral branch from Boscarne Junction to Wenford Bridge.

No 6024 *King Edward I* leaves Bodmin General on 23 May 1998, for a brief trip to Town! *John Stretton*

Diesel stock includes Class 08 and 10 shunters, Class 33 No 33110, Class 37 No 37142, Class 47 No 47303 and Class 50 No 50042. Former industrial locomotives include a pair of ex-Port of Par Bagnall 0-4-0STs, 0-4-0ST No 19 built by Bagnall in 1951 (one of two locos earlier held by the Great Western Society at Bodmin motive power depot in 1972), a Ruston Hornsby 0-4-0 shunter and Hunslet Austerity 0-6-0ST No 2766.

Cholsey & Wallingford Railway

O riginally conceived in 1861 as an independent route from Moulsford to Princes Risborough by way of Wallingford and Watlington, the plan was amended in 1863 to run from a junction with the GWR near Cholsey. From there, the Wallingford & Watlington Railway opened in 1866 but never reached Watlington, instead terminating at Wallingford. It was sold to the GWR in 1872.

The branch operated until 1959, when it was closed to passenger traffic, although freight into the old Wallingford station continued until 1965, and traffic serving the maltings on the outskirts of the town continued until 1981. It was at this time that the Cholsey & Wallingford Railway Preservation Society was formed to save the line as a heritage railway and tourist attraction.

Cholsey station has a branch platform still available to the preserved railway and this offers connection with the national rail network in the form of the Great Western Main Line between Reading and Didcot. At the other end of the

Class 08 No 08022 *Lion* stands in Cholsey station, alongside the FGW main line, after arriving from Wallingford on 3 July 2005. *John Stretton*

2½ miles of track, the original Wallingford station is no more, but a makeshift facility and the railway's headquarters are situated next to the site of the maltings that kept the branch open into the preservation era.

The preserved Cholsey & Wallingford Railway opened to the public in 1985, though it was 1997 before a regular advertised service over the full length of the line was available. Most services are diesel-hauled, with the railway's ex-BR Class 08 shunter being used on most trains. Trains run on some weekends between Easter and Christmas, and on Bank Holidays, with steam operation on special event days when visiting locomotives take charge of the trains.

The line runs from the bay at Cholsey station, which remains largely intact and as it was when originally built, through the fields of south Oxfordshire and over farm crossings before arriving at the historic riverside town of Wallingford.

Port Talbot 0-6-0ST No 26 became GWR No 813, and while now based on the Severn Valley Railway this sturdy little workhorse has visited many locations since first steaming in preservation (in 2000). Here No 813 is handling the shuttle to Cholsey on 28 May 2006, complete with 'The Bunk' headboard, awaiting the next trip up the line. *John Stretton*

Displaying their 'Guinness' livery, No 08060 *Unicorn* and No 08022 *Lion* stand in the platform at Wallingford on 2 October 2004. *John Stretton*

Visiting Hunslet WD 0-6-0ST No 10 *Cumbria* is seen out in the country with a good head of steam on a very dull 21 November 2009. *Cliff Thomas*

Dean Forest Railway

The Dean Forest Railway Preservation Society exists to create a working example of the once extensive railway system in the Forest of Dean. The section is the last remaining part of the Severn & Wye Railway from Lydney Town to Parkend, in the Royal Forest of Dean National Park.

When it was rumoured in 1970 that the line was to be closed by BR (as by then only the occasional coal and stone ballast traffic was being worked), the Dean Forest Railway Company was formed. First a siding at Parkend was leased from BR, then the overgrown site of an old mine at Norchard, north of Lydney, and later the adjoining derelict area that had been the site of Lydney power station, were acquired. Planning consent for the Preservation Centre was granted in 1975, but because of the extensive clearance work involved it was January 1978 before the locos and other vehicles formerly stored at Parkend could be moved to their new home at the Norchard Steam Centre, which opened to the public at Easter of that year.

Although traffic had ceased between Lydney and Parkend in 1976, the single line was

Above: Norchard (Low Level) is a delightful setting, here on a fine and sunny 7 April 2007, '5700' Class 0-6-0PT No 9681 climbs into the terminus with a four coach train from Lydney Junction. *Peter Townsend*

Left: The following day Class 108 DMU No M56492 arrives from Parkend at Norchard's High Level platform with a service to Lydney Junction. *Peter Townsend*

In between trains author and retired Dean Forest railwayman Bob Barnett (centre) discusses the finer points of his book *Dean Forest Footplate Memories* with the signalmen at Norchard during the 2007 Gala. *Peter Townsend*

'The Cambrian Coast Express', alias the 1415 Lydney Junction-Parkend passenger turn during the DFR's 'Severn & Wye Railway Festival 2010', celebrating 200 years of the S&WR, arrives at Parkend behind Nos 5521 and 3717 *City of Truro* on Sunday 27 June 2010. *John Stretton*

not officially declared closed until the latter part of 1980, whereupon negotiations could begin to purchase the branch from BR. Complex legal problems had to be overcome before the contract for the purchase of the 4-mile branch was finally signed with BR in November 1983.

The Norchard Steam Centre, created as it was from two derelict industrial sites, was by 1984 one of the most picturesque of its kind, surrounded by woodland and with an original Severn & Wye Railway building (from Drybrook Road station) and the signal box from Gloucester Mileage Yard. A running line with a gradient of 1 in 40 in places passes the site and gives a good grandstand view.

By 1984 the society had amassed an impressive collection of passenger rolling stock and wagons, together with motive power that included GWR '4575' 2-6-2T No 5541, '57XX' 0-6-0PT No 9681, rescued from Woodham's scrapyard at Barry, and Class '5101' 2-6-2T No 4121, another ex-Barry loco, while the next arrival was 'Hall' 4-6-0 No 4953 *Pitchford Hall*. At that time the society's star performer was Hunslet 'Austerity' 0-6-0ST No 3806, aided by Peckett 0-4-0ST No 2147 *Uskmouth 1*.

More recently the Dean Forest Railway has acquired the former GWR signal box from near Codsall station in Staffordshire, now to adorn Whitecroft station, one of the society's five stops along the line from Parkend to Lydney Junction, where connection can be made with the national network line between Gloucester and Newport, a distance of 4¼ miles, and plans are being formulated to extend a further 2½ miles into the middle of the Royal Forest.

Derwent Valley Railway

The Derwent Valley Light Railway was a privately owned route from Layerthorpe, on the outskirts of the city of York, to Cliffe Common near Selby, forming a 16-mile freight line. It owed its existence to the Light Railways Act of 1896, which allowed the farming communities to the south-east of York to approach the Rural District Councils of Escrick and Riccall with a view to building a line with the purpose of linking them directly into the markets at York and Selby. Though both Councils initially agreed to support the scheme, they both subsequently withdrew their support as costs soared, leaving the landowners themselves to fund the railway by means of a share subscription. Unique among standard-gauge light railways in this country, the DVLR escaped both the 1923 'Grouping' and the 1948 nationalisation, to remain privately owned throughout its working life.

Above: The 'steam train trips' day on Saturday 9 October 1976 featured LNWR No 790 *Hardwicke* hauling several trains between York's Layerthorpe station and Dunnington, a distance of about 4 miles, and certainly attracted an appreciative audience.

Left and below: There being no turning facility for the loco, *Hardwicke* had to run round her train, while her fireman sees to the coal in her tender, then she's off to Dunnington again.

Dating from 1913, the route could be said to start as a branch off the York-Scarborough line at Burton Lane signal box, though this is actually the BR Foss Islands branch. Further along this branch, past Rowntree's Factory Halt, the

On the final run to
Dunnington on the
'steam train trips' day
of Saturday 9 October
1976, *Hardwicke*'s crew
give her her head out of
Layerthorpe station.

The three-year project to
operate regular summer
services fell to ex-NER
tank loco *Joem*, but never
attracted the crowds in
sufficient numbers. *Joem*
was built by BR as late
as 1951, an amazing
53 years after the first
members of designer
William Worsdell's
class were introduced in
1898. Designated power
class 2F and carrying
the number 69023, the
loco was sold as BR
Experimental Number
59 during 1966, when
its new owner, Ron
Ainsworth, named it
Joem in memory of
his father Joseph and
mother Emmeline, and
restored it to NER livery.
Here she awaits her next
run to Dunnington on
30 August 1979.

DVLR proper branches again to its true
beginnings at Layerthorpe station, once
advertised as 'York's other railway station'.
Layerthorpe was the largest station on
the line, the company's HQ and the site
of the engine shed. The route went on to
Osbaldwick, Murton Lane, Dunnington,
Elvington, Wheldrake, Cottingwith,
Thorganby, Skipwith and finally Cliffe
Common Junction for connection to
Selby via the BR line from Market
Weighton. Surprisingly, there was not
a single signal box along the entire
length of the line; in fact, the only signal
originally installed was at Wheldrake,
where a sharp bend just before the station
obscured the sight of the level crossing
and a warning to the driver was therefore
needed, the signal being operated by the
opening and closing of the level crossing
gates.

At first, both passenger and freight
traffic was encouraging, but the passenger
usage declined dramatically in the early
1920s as bus services spread into the
countryside, and passenger services were
ended in 1926. Goods traffic continued
to increase throughout the 1930s and, as
the threat of war loomed, the Government made increasing use of the line in
preparation for the impending conflict. The war years proved to be the busiest
period for the DVLR as it supplied the large number of military bases in the area,
as well as transporting vital agricultural produce. A lack of track maintenance
resulted in the line being overgrown with weeds, so much so that it was virtually
invisible to the enemy's aerial photography!

The Selby to Driffield line, of which the Market Weighton branch was part,
was closed by BR in 1964 as part of the Beeching cuts, thus isolating the DVLR,
and successive sections were then closed due to lack of traffic, until by 1973 only
about 4 miles from Layerthorpe to Dunnington remained operative. With the
closure of the company's last major source of freight, Yorkshire Grain Driers Ltd
at Dunnington, the line
was doomed, in spite of
an attempt by the owners
of the independent
freight-only line to join
forces with the newly
opened National Railway
Museum to revive its
fortunes by using NER
Class 'J72' 0-6-0 tank
Joem and ex-LNWR
'Precedent' Class No 790
Hardwicke to haul special
passenger trains. York's
local newspaper, the
Yorkshire Evening Press,

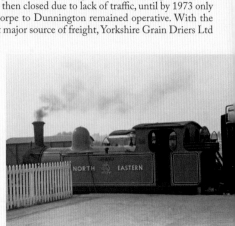

heralded the venture on 9 September 1976 with the headline 'Steam train trips from York planned', and went on to describe how the trains would use rolling stock from the NRM hauled initially by *Hardwicke* and possibly connecting with the NRM by means of a vintage bus such as an open-topped charabanc. Following a successful test run a week later, a day of 'steam train trips' was organised for 9 October, when three runs were made in each direction to test the viability of a summer tourist service the next year. The result was described as 'very encouraging' in the *Evening Press* of 11 October, with 300 passengers being carried.

Encouraged by this success, trains ran regularly from the summer of 1977, hauled to Dunnington by *Joem*. Leaving Layerthorpe at 2.30pm and returning at 3.30pm, the venture never really became a financial success, largely because Layerthorpe station is just a little too far from York city centre to be conveniently accessible. The directors unsuccessfully sought to negotiate with BR to run the company's trains over the Foss Islands link into York station, so a bus service link into the city was necessary, but sadly by the end of 1979 the Derwent Valley line was finally closed, the track lifted and *Joem* transferred to the North Yorkshire Moors Railway to continue working, though now repainted in BR livery and carrying her BR number 69023. Traffic from the Rowntree factory kept the York end of the Foss Islands branch open for a time, but that too eventually succumbed and was closed in the late 1980s. The section from Burton Lane Junction to Osbaldwick is now a cycle track.

The Foss Islands branch continued to be operated by BR until 1989, when closure finally ended the era – but that was not the end of the line for the tenacious Derwent Valley Light Railway. Although much of the route was sold for redevelopment, the half-mile to the west of Murton Lane station had been taken over by the Yorkshire Museum of Farming, whose Murton Park site was next to the line. Sensing an opportunity, enthusiasts negotiated the donation of *Churchill*, one of the shunters from the former Yorkshire Grain Driers site at Dunnington, to the museum, and in 1985 the Light Railway Order was transferred to the Yorkshire Museum's section of line. Later, in August 1990, the Great Yorkshire Preservation Society transferred its operations to the museum from its former base at the old NER Starbeck steam shed near Harrogate, whereupon members carried out considerable restoration work on the line and began to build up a collection of locomotives and rolling stock. Most impressive was the dismantling, movement and re-erection on the museum site of the former DVLR station building from Wheldrake, which had been converted into a bungalow but had stood empty for 20 years.

As if in recognition of the unerring dedication of the enthusiasts involved in this labour of love over the 12 years since the DVLR's demise, permission was granted in 1993 to operate under the name of the 'Derwent Valley Light Railway' once again and, needless to say, plans are afoot to improve and extend into the future.

Top: One of the surviving freight services from the Foss Islands branch joins the Scarborough-York line at Burton Lane Junction on 24 August 1981, with an 08 shunter in charge. Note the NER lower-quadrant semaphore signal.

Above: On the same day, a DMU waits to collect workers from Rowntree's Factory Halt.

Didcot Railway Centre

It was in 1967 that BR ended the use of its loco depot at Didcot and offered it to the recently restructured preservation group calling itself the Great Western Society, to become its principal restoration centre and allowing it to gather the majority of its stock under cover, albeit in a very limited manner. The site is a crescent-shaped piece of land 1,200 yards long by 150 yards wide, lying between two BR routes from London to Oxford (one passing through the station, the other diverging north-westwards to pass the station and rejoin the other, earlier route at Didcot North Junction). It has no road access, though this seeming disadvantage brought with it the bonus of reduced possibilities for vandalism and theft!

The choice of Didcot as the headquarters for the GWS was dictated by expediency – by what was available, the area from which it drew its membership, and by hard cash. Nevertheless it was a good choice, being less than an hour's journey by rail from London or Bristol, not much more than that from Birmingham, and very close indeed to the 'Mecca' of all GWR believers – Swindon. Conveniently, the site is next to BR's Didcot station in rural Oxfordshire and proved to be an ideal location, with workshops and covered accommodation for the stock, and alongside Brunel's main line. Originally, however, only about half of the site could be occupied by the society as the rest was a wasteland of grass and scrub still controlled by BR. In spite of this, open days had been held since 1971 and the society's 650-yard 'Demonstration Track' had proved popular with visitors.

GWR 'Modified Hall' No 6998 *Burton Agnes Hall* poses for the cameras.

The first tangible result of the society's development observable to the 'outside world' was probably the inaugural run on the BR main line of its fully restored vintage train, which took place on 19 October 1974. Headed by the GWS's own motive power in the shape of 5MT 'Manor' 4-6-0 No 7808 *Cookham Manor* double-headed with 5MT 'Modified Hall' 4-6-0 No 6998 *Burton Agnes Hall*, the train of seven restored GWR coaches ran from Didcot to Stratford-upon-Avon, where the locomotives were turned and later continued with their train to Tyseley for servicing and to enable passengers to visit the Birmingham Railway Museum. *Cookham Manor* was making its first outing since undergoing a heavy overhaul at Didcot, which had taken more than two years. The seven coaches included 'Ocean Saloon' No 9118, built in 1932 for ocean liner traffic between Plymouth and Paddington, 3rd Class Open Saloon No 1289, built in 1937 for excursion service, and five compartment vehicles all with traditional GWR features painstakingly restored by the GWS's talented and skilful team.

Before being allowed to run on BR metals, the coaches had to undergo stringent mechanical and electrical examinations, which included lifting them off the bogies, testing the vacuum braking, steam heating and electrical systems, and even ultrasonic examination of the axles.

By 1976 agreement had been reached for the society to extend into the full area of the site and thus expand its operations over some 16 acres. A

'5700' Class 0-6-0PT No 3738 hauls its train over the demonstration track to provide rides for the visitors.

comprehensive development plan could now be drawn up that would include a carriage restoration and storage shed, overhaul of the locomotive shed building, a second demonstration line to be linked to an extension of the original, giving an operating length of some 1,100 yards, with typical GWR buildings on both sections. The ambitious plans also included a 'mushroom' water tower, signal box, turntable and a length of 'mixed gauge' track to demonstrate the historical need to transfer freight between 'standard gauge' and 'broad gauge' lines. By 1977 much progress had been made on several of these projects, and visitors could witness the developments as well as seeing restoration of locomotives and rolling stock, as the depot had been open regularly with engines in steam from Easter through to October.

These facilities allowed the Great Western Society to rescue several large locos from Barry scrapyard, even though they were in poor condition with parts missing, yet still giving a good chance of being able to return them to working order. In the early 1970s the society's ex-GWR loco stock included 4-6-0s Nos 5051 *Earl Bathurst*, 5900 *Hinderton Hall*, 6998 *Burton Agnes Hall* and 7808 *Cookham Manor*, together with 2-6-2T No 6106, 0-6-2T No 6687, 0-6-0PT No 3650, 0-4-2T No 1466 and 0-4-0ST No 1340, the latter dating way back to 1897! Other locos on loan to the society, such as LNER 'A2' No 60532 *Blue Peter*, together with its impressive collection of coaches and other rolling stock, were helping establish Didcot as an important working railway centre in a typical GWR location, with much thought having gone into the whole activity and atmosphere. What Didcot lacks in terms of track-length, it certainly makes up for in terms of classic locomotive designs.

By 1981 the society was promoted as the Didcot Railway

'Manor' Class No 7808 *Cookham Manor* stands outside the sheds.

Above: Inside the sheds, 'Hall' Class No 5900 *Hinderton Hall* receives attention.

Above right: 0-6-0ST No 1363 stands outside, alongside *Cookham Manor.*

Centre and work was well advanced on the second demonstration line. Much improved visitor facilities were added, including greater catering capacity, modern toilets, shop and 'small relics' museum, to better display the society's vast collection of hardware, print and publicity items. This latter was formally opened by John Craven of BBC TV's *Newsround* fame on August Bank Holiday 1982. Its aim is to show the GWR as much more than a series of locomotives and trains moving people from A to B. For the workforce it was a way of life, for many a family tradition, and most of all the company excelled in a pride in its standards, exemplified perhaps to extremes in its almost manic determination to mark with its name every item it produced. These pieces form the basis of the collection in the small relics museum – cutlery, clothing, spanners, garden tools, trolleys, paperweights, stamps books and even pen nibs. Soap, scissors, watches, waste-paper baskets, hinges, locks, stretchers – anything and everything bearing the company's name, letters or crest finds a home here. Needless to say, private donations have added to the already impressive collection and plans are afoot to broaden and extend the facility to further illustrate to visitors the impact of railways on all aspects of their lives.

It's not all GWR at Didcot, as this ex-SR 'Pacific' shows. Representing the Southern Railway, 'Battle of Britain' Class 4-6-2 No 34051 *Winston Churchill* stands proudly outside the engine sheds.

The centre, which the society describes as 'an authentic fragment of the old GWR', now boasts an original four-road engine shed dating from the 1930s, lifting shop, ash shed and 75,000-gallon water tower, as well as a turntable, coaling stage and replica GWR station to go with its recreation of Brunel's 'broad-gauge' (7ft 0¼in) and standard-gauge tracks. Both of these short lengths have a station at each end, though the term is perhaps a little grand in the case of the broad-gauge line, with its 'Halt' at one end and the old 1869 vintage 'transhipment shed' at the other. This shed was used originally to transfer goods from standard-gauge to broad-gauge rolling stock and vice versa, by man-handling everything across an intermediate platform – a time-consuming operation that was abandoned in 1892 together with the broad gauge. Thankfully the shed and its tracks remained intact, and when the GWS arrived at Didcot its historical importance was realised and it was also preserved.

East Lancashire Railway

The East Lancashire Railway was opened in 1846 as a link from the Manchester to Bolton line, and became busy with both passenger services and freight along the Irwell Valley from Bury to Rawtenstall, as part of the Lancashire & Yorkshire Railway. The undoubted benefits to the local industries, including mining, quarrying and of course the cotton mill empires, were the driving force behind the promotion of the new railways, but passenger services soon became a significant source of income, as the draw of Manchester and other large towns in the area attracted the local population. The Irwell Valley had proved an ideal location for cotton spinning, with its damp atmosphere (cotton threads break easily when too dry) and plentiful water power to supply the new mills. Production had quickly blossomed from cottage industry to major manufacturing, housed in large purpose-built mills powered first by water, then by steam. The inadequate roads and canals of the area led the mill-owners of the 1840s to demand better transport connections to Manchester and beyond, and that meant being on the railway map.

The East Lancashire Railway system initially developed around Bury, superseding the canal built in 1796, which linked the town with Manchester. The Manchester, Bolton & Bury Canal Navigation & Railway was incorporated in 1831, but never did build the much-sought-after railway. It would be the subsequent Manchester, Bury & Rossendale Railway that would produce a scheme in 1844 not only to link Manchester and Bury, but would extend the railway north of Bury to the mills of Rossendale. Although the Act authorising the construction was obtained, the MB&RR was absorbed into the East Lancashire Railway Company on 21 July 1845.

Initially there were in fact two separate railways that would eventually become the one we know today as the East Lancs. The north-south route (as promoted in 1844 by the Manchester, Bury & Rossendale Railway) comprising a branch from the Manchester to Bolton line at Clifton Junction, running then via Radcliffe to Bury, then along the Irwell Valley through Summerseat, Ramsbottom, Rossendale, Ewood Bridge and on to Rawtenstall. This became part of the original East Lancashire Railway, from which today's heritage line gets its name. The line was later extended in 1848 from Stubbins Junction, just north of Ramsbottom, to Accrington, while the Rossendale branch was extended in 1852 as far as Bacup. Predating this was the east-west route, opened in 1841, which was a branch of the Manchester & Leeds Railway from Blue Pitts, south of Castleton, to Heywood, later itself extended to Bury in 1848, by which time the Manchester & Leeds Railway, together with several others on both sides of the Pennines, had amalgamated to form the fledgling Lancashire & Yorkshire. In 1859, after only 13 years of existence, the East Lancashire Railway was also incorporated into the growing L&YR empire, although in those volatile times of railway expansion even the L&YR itself would be swallowed up to become part of the London & North Western Railway in 1922. A year later the 'Grouping' of 1923 would see the LNWR disappear into the London Midland & Scottish

At Rawtenstall station on 22 September 1991, shortly after the East Lancashire Railway had extended its line, ex-War Department 'Austerity' 0-6-0ST No 193 *Shropshire* heads a train from Bury. Almost 500 of these locos were built between 1943 and 1953. Although most were passed to industrial users to work in docks, or to the National Coal Board, where their short wheelbase was ideal for negotiating tight curves, 75 were bought by the LNER in 1946 and classified 'J94'. Later classified 4F by BR, they were eventually withdrawn between 1960 and 1967 and a few were sold into industrial use, such as to the NCB, to rejoin their 'classmates'.

Ivatt LMS Class 2MT No 46443 prepares to leave Ramsbottom station on 23 January 2011.

Pausing with her return train on the same day, No 46443 is joined by BR Standard Class 5MT No 73129.

Railway, which, together with the Southern, Great Western and London & North Eastern companies, would form the so-called 'Big Four', which remained in existence for the next 25 years until nationalisation amalgamated them into British Railways in 1948.

In common with much of the national railway network, most lines in the former L&YR area were in a seriously run-down condition after the Second World War. That, combined with the rapid expansion of the fast-improving road transport system, sounded the death knell for many a cherished branch line, so it came as no great surprise (though nonetheless a bitter blow) that the publication on 27 March 1963 of Dr Beeching's infamous report, *The Reshaping of British Railways*, proposed that the services to Bury by way of the former East Lancs route should be among those to be withdrawn. The stretch of line from Rawtenstall to Bacup was closed to traffic on 5 December 1966, the tracks being lifted shortly afterwards. The Accrington branch fell to the axe on the same date.

The last passenger train along the Bury to Rawtenstall line ran in 1972, and as mills closed in the area so freight traffic dwindled and the line inevitably closed in 1982. By this time, however, plans had been developing for many years to save the railway, and when the new Bury Bus-Rail Interchange was opened in 1980 it paved the way for discussions centred around the now defunct Bolton Street station. The possibility of reopening the Bury to Rawtenstall line became a reality. By February 1983 the track had still not been lifted. At this time the Greater Manchester Council (GMC) was actively involved in promoting recreation in the area, with the Croal-Irwell Valley Reclamation Programme serving as a focal point. The potential benefits of opening a preserved steam railway within this heavily populated conurbation were enormous, not only for the Bury area, but also as a means by which the great industrial heritage of the North West of England could be explored.

The East Lancs Railway Preservation Society (ELRPS) had been formed in 1968 and moved to Bury in 1972, whereupon work began in earnest to preserve part of the line, focussing on the Bury to Rawtenstall section. Bury's Bolton Street station was the starting point, even though for the next eight years there was no accurate idea of exactly when the line would eventually be closed. Securing an ex-East Lancashire Railway warehouse, built in 1848, as its

headquarters was an early step along the road to rebuilding the railway. By the early 1980s the warehouse had become the Bury Transport Museum and home to a fledgling collection of locomotives and rolling stock. With help from local authorities in the area, coordinated by the GMC, it was possible to purchase the track, trackbed and all the infrastructure from BR, financed mainly by Derelict Land Grants. Early stock on the railway was limited to Barclay 0-4-0ST No 1927 and 0-6-0T No 7683, together with an MR truck and a four-wheel goods van.

Early inhabitants of the Transport Museum included rebuilt 'West Country' 'Pacific' No 34027 *Taw Valley*, ex BR diesel-hydraulics Nos D1041 *Western Prince* and D832 *Onslaught*, and six industrial steam locomotives. The society by this time had also taken possession of a number of coaches, wagons and a steam crane built by Craven Bros of Loughborough in 1950 and recently retired from Carlisle Kingmoor. *Taw Valley* had arrived by road from the North Yorkshire Moors Railway on 24 November 1982 for restoration at the museum. The four coaches, three wagons and the steam crane had arrived by rail on the night of 26 August. All had then been shunted through the still disused Bolton Street station to the society's headquarters by its 0-6-0 tank No 70 *Phoenix* (Hudswell Clarke No 1464 of 1921 vintage).

Some months previously, on 27 March 1982, the society, in conjunction with the GMC, organised three BR eight-car DMU 'specials' to run the length of the branch to test public reaction to the possible reopening of the line. The 'East Lancashire Phoenix', as the specials were called, were a total success, and fully sold out, with many hundreds more people turning out to watch the event and to visit the museum. With this success behind them, the ELRPS was further inspired and motivated to forge ahead with its goal of breathing life back into the Bury to Rawtenstall line.

The first passenger trains ran on 25 July 1987 along 4 miles of track between Bury and Ramsbottom, and 35,000 fare-payers travelled on the railway in that short season, almost doubling to 60,000 in 1988 and continuing to go from strength to strength in the following years. The line was extended to Rawtenstall in 1991, eventually giving about 12 miles of mainly uphill running, all the way from Bury into the Lancashire countryside.

As passenger numbers increased, with longer trains to be hauled up some testing gradients, more pulling power was clearly needed, and the ELR progressively increased its stock of more powerful locomotives, including an LMS 5MT 'Black 5'. This would be the shape of things to come, as within a few short years the list of steam

'Black 5' No 44871 manoeuvres her train at the platform, before heading for Bury over Summerseat Viaduct on 23 January 2011.

BR Class 8P 4-6-2 No 71000 *Duke of Gloucester* makes a fine sight crossing Summerseat Viaduct on the same day while heading for Ramsbottom.

locomotives that called this stretch of line in the old county of Lancashire their home included three LMS 'Black 5s', Nos 44871, 45337 and 45407 *The Lancashire Fusilier*, LMS 'Crab' No 42765, and LMS Ivatt 2MT No 46428. Added to these were GWR 2-8-0 No 3855 and 2-8-2T No 7229, SR 'Battle of Britain' Class No 34073 *249 Squadron* and 'Merchant Navy' No 35009 *Shaw Savill*, and LNER 'B12/2' 4-6-0 No 61572, not forgetting BR 4MT 2-6-4T No 80097 and the unique 4-6-2 8P No 71000 *Duke of Gloucester* – an impressive stock list by any standard, and one that does not include the 'industrials'.

In recent years a major project for the ELR has been the extension to Heywood, thereby connecting with the national network. After a prolonged period involving the overcoming of complex legal and statutory problems, the Bury to Heywood section was finally opened to passenger services on 6 September 2003, with a further short length of 500 metres beyond the newly built Heywood station over Green Lane level crossing to Hapwood allowing locomotive and stock interchange with the national network to be completed.

No 46443 heads out into the country at Ewood Bridge.

In the light of its growing popularity and steadily increasing passenger numbers, a further development is planned to extend the ELR to Castleton, on the Manchester Victoria to Bradford and Leeds route via the Calder Valley, and consultations are ongoing with Rochdale Council with a view to accomplishing this.

The railway operates every weekend and Bank Holiday throughout the year, with the exception of Christmas Day, with mid-week services running on Wednesdays, Thursdays and Fridays from May to September, at Easter and during October half-term.

Embsay & Bolton Abbey Railway

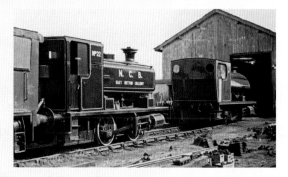

The Embsay & Bolton Abbey Railway, run by the Yorkshire Dales Railway Museum Trust, centred at Embsay near Skipton, began to attract attention with its fleet of industrial locos and dreams of extending its empire the 4 miles down the valley to the busy tourist attraction of Bolton Abbey, as well as into the bustling market town of Skipton, known as the 'Gateway to the Dales', there to link with BR's Airedale line. Operating over part of the Midland Railway's line from Skipton to Ilkley, opened in 1888 and closed by BR in 1965, the Yorkshire Dales Railway Society was formed in 1969 and activity began at the Embsay site in 1970 to establish the headquarters and install the first locomotive, Hudswell Clarke 0-4-0ST *Nellie*, an oil-fired steam industrial on loan from Bradford Corporation, for which she had worked since her introduction at Esholt Sewage Works in 1922.

Two of the Yorkshire Dales Railway's industrial 0-4-0s on shed at Embsay during March 1980, including Barclay No 22 from the National Coal Board's East Hetton Colliery.

Initially named the Embsay & Grassington Railway Preservation Society and formed in 1968, its primary aim was to preserve the historically important and then threatened Yorkshire Dales Railway branch from Skipton to Grassington. This closure never did take place and the branch still carries significant quantities of much-sought-after local stone. A change of name to the Yorkshire Dales Railway Society in 1969 saw the impetus focus upon preserving something of the character of the old Midland Railway in the area, with a plan to reopen part of the closed Skipton to Ilkley line and to concentrate efforts on the now derelict Embsay station, which had no power supply and had been oil-lit. At first, the YDRS had to be content to rent the station until funds could be raised to purchase the land and adjacent track, but a 'steam centre' plan was

Embsay's signal box, a beautifully restored Midland Railway original, is seen in 1982, and controlling train movements around the station.

0-6-0ST *Slough Estates
No 5*, built in 1939,
receives attention at
Embsay during March
1980.

quickly formulated and a simple railway operation was introduced, involving
a couple of former Manchester South Junction & Altrincham electric railway
trailer cars sandwiched between two steam locomotives, and augmented with a
small collection of trolleybuses.

Open days followed as the society collected more locos and traction engines
to provide the growing number of visitors with a unique and interesting array
of former industrial locomotives and related stock operating from the station,
with its original signal box and 4,400 yards of track. Eventually, in 1979 Embsay
station was refurbished and reopened in LMS condition, with a loop-line to
the west of the station to allow locos to run round their trains. The centre had
a growing collection of industrial steam locos, mainly of the 0-4-0ST and
0-6-0ST designs, more than 20 in number by the early 1980s. For marketing
purposes and to confirm the railway's location and purpose, the name Embsay
Steam Railway was subsequently adopted, together with plans to extend the
line along the valley to the important tourist attraction of Bolton Abbey, with
its 12th-century priory located in the valley of the beautiful River Wharfe. This
represents a major project, involving as it does the reinstatement of two bridges,
the reclamation of 2 miles of trackbed, and the construction of the track itself,
not forgetting another derelict station to rebuild as the railway's terminus, giving

Now in full working
order, she runs round her
train at Embsay station on
a mild and sunny January
day in 1982.

passengers a 4-mile journey in the lovely Yorkshire Dales.

One of the smaller preservation groups, describing itself as 'a living museum of Britain's industrial railways', the YDR has among its locomotive stock such rarities as *City Link*, the only remaining working example of a locomotive built by the Yorkshire Engine Company of Sheffield, while its coaching stock includes examples of Gresley 'Control Train' coaches. 'Control Trains' were part of the secret world of the railways and date back to 1953, when the Government was still concerned about and planning for the eventuality of any future hostilities that might necessitate the moving of the District Control Offices and the construction of replacement Emergency Control Centres. Consequently, the six railway regions then in being were each provided with two of these 'hush-hush' trains. Those for the North Eastern Region and Eastern Region each consisted of two types of coaches: Open 2nds to LNER Diagram 186 and Corridor 2nds to LNER Diagram 115. Two of each type formed each train, together with a Generator Car equipped with two diesel generators, and a Stores Car and Mess Car. The four trains were stabled at York and Newcastle (for the NER) and at Retford (for the ER). In the event of an emergency requiring their deployment, they would be moved to pre-planned sites where all the necessary facilities had been provided. These sites were at Darlington for the Newcastle-based train and Hebden Bridge for the York set. One Retford train would remain on site while the other would be deployed in the Eastern Counties.

It was not until July 1979 that a decision was finally taken by the Department of Transport to withdraw these Government-sponsored secret trains, so the 16 coaches making up the four Eastern Region trains (the NER had been merged into the ER in 1967) were officially condemned. After the removal of various items of equipment, they were put up for disposal by BR. Six of the ER Gresley Control Coaches were sold to a breaker, C. F. Booth of Rotherham, for scrap, but the rest were saved. Of these, one found a new home on the North Yorkshire Moors Railway, three went to the Severn Valley Railway, two were purchased and put into store by Resco Railways Ltd, one is housed at Carnforth awaiting restoration, and three were acquired for the Yorkshire Dales Railway and moved there in 1981, with a fourth example being expected to join them soon, possibly one of the Resco purchases.

Only minor repairs were needed to the YDR coaches, which are of the Diagram 186 'Tourist Open 2nd' design, and it was hoped to have them in service within the year, when one would have been converted for use as a buffet car, leaving the others in their original form. The YDR examples on site during 1981 were from the Retford trains: Departmental Nos TDE 321001 (LNER No 43654), TDE 321002 (LNER 52256) and TDE 321006 (LNER 43636), all built in 1935.

Ready to take her train forward from Embsay in April 1982, regular workhorse *Slough Estates No 5* poses for the camera. The Slough Estates Railway had ceased operation on 27 April 1973.

By 1983, six Mark I coaches had been purchased from BR and delivered over the newly installed link with British Rail laid jointly by BR and YDR personnel at Embsay Junction, where connection had been established with BR's line between Skipton and Grassington in 1981. Though much depends on the future of the Grassington branch, this new rail link to the 'outside world' brings the possibility of running steam trains into the bustling market town of Skipton, with its important station, on the 'steam specials' routes to Carnforth and over the famous Settle & Carlisle line.

More than just a railway, the Embsay & Bolton Abbey Railway promotes a programme of activities that it hopes will form an essential ingredient in the attraction of the Yorkshire Dales and of the Skipton area in particular. These include crafts, cycling, vintage road vehicles, 'real food' and 'real ale', model engineering and model railways. Industrial archaeology weekends are also being pioneered and the station shop has built up a large trade in books on the subject, specialising in titles from smaller publishers.

Meet 'Thomas and Friends', in the form of Hunslet 0-6-0ST No S121 *Primrose No 2*, saved from the Primrose Hill Colliery, Leeds, and a Barclay 0-4-0ST from the National Coal Board's East Hetton Colliery, both seen at Embsay station on a wet winter weekend in 1982.

GLOUCESTERSHIRE WARWICKSHIRE RAILWAY

The Gloucestershire Warwickshire Railway (G/WR) operates over a 12-mile section of the former Great Western Railway's Cheltenham-Stratford-upon-Avon-Birmingham line, known as the 'Honeybourne Line', built between 1900 and 1906. The original section was opened by the Oxford, Worcester & Wolverhampton Railway in 1859 and acquired by the GWR in 1883. The line was run down over the years and finally closed in 1976. The section operated by the G/WR is between Laverton Halt and Cheltenham Racecourse stations.

The Gloucestershire Warwickshire Steam Railway plc was formed in 1981, when track-laying began. A Light Railway Order, which allowed the laying of up to 15 miles of track, was granted in 1983.

Officially opened by Nicholas Ridley MP, Secretary of State for Transport, in 1984, the first train ran from Toddington over 700 yards of track. Journeys were extended to 5 miles by 1994, and now 12 miles of track have been restored. Winchcombe station has been recreated, and the latest extension to Cheltenham Race Course station, completed in 2002, was opened by HRH The Princess Royal on 7 April 2003, thereby once again fulfilling its original purpose of bringing race-goers for important meetings such as the Cheltenham Gold Cup.

The railway currently has three operational steam locomotives, GWR '2800' Class 2-8-0 No 2807, officially the oldest loco to have been rescued from Barry scrapyard, LMS 8F 2-8-0 No 45160, repatriated from Turkey in the 1980s, and GWR 'Modified Hall' 4-6-0 No 7903 *Foremarke Hall*.

Several other steam locos are undergoing restoration, repair or overhaul, including GWR 'Modified Hall' Nos 6960 *Raveningham Hall* and 6984 *Owsden Hall*, SR 'Merchant Navy' Class 4-6-2 No 35006 *Peninsular & Oriental S. N. Co*, GWR 0-6-0PT No 9642, GWR 2-8-0T No 4270, and LMS 4F 0-6-0 No 44027. The society also operates a number of ex-BR diesel locomotives including Class 03 shunters Nos D2069 and D2184, Class 20 No D8137, Class 24 No 24081, Class 37 Nos 37215 and 37324, Class 47 Nos 47105 and 47376, and Class 73 No 73129. There is also a substantial collection of ex-BR Mk 1 coaches, an Observation Car and Bullion Van.

The railway runs services at weekends and on Tuesdays, Wednesdays and Thursdays during the week, over the current

'Modified Hall' 4-6-0 No 7903 *Foremarke Hall* storms out of Greet Tunnel, on the approach to Winchcombe station, with empty stock from Cheltenham Racecourse, on 17 November 2007. *John Stretton*

Right: In a wonderful recreation of bygone times, '4500' Class No 5542 leaves Toddington with the 1450 Auto shuttle to Winchcombe, during the G/WR's four-day gala on Friday 1 June 2007. *John Stretton*

Bottom right: Is this 1957? A remarkable recreation of a branch line train of half a decade ago, seen on Saturday, 17 November 2007! With steam to spare, No 65462 stands in Winchcombe station on, during a Steam Team charter, waiting for its next load of passengers. *John Stretton*

Above and below: The occasion is the rededication of 9F 2-10-0 No 92203 *Black Prince.* Owner David Shepherd shares a joke with Alan Titchmarsh at Toddington station on 18 October 2004. *John Stretton*

12 miles from Laverton, through Toddington and Winchcombe to Cheltenham Race Course. When the northern extension to Broadway is completed – the target date for this, including rebuilding the station, being 2015 – the operational line will be 15 miles long.

In addition to improved facilities in the form of the Flag & Whistle Tea Rooms at Toddington station, a 1950s-style coffee shop at Winchcombe and on-train buffet services, the line also features the second-longest tunnel on a heritage railway, the 693-yard Greet Tunnel, south of Winchcombe station (which is also reputed to be haunted!). Following this experience, the line emerges onto an embankment that affords excellent views over the Vale of Evesham to the distant Malvern Hills.

The railway was presented with the Ian Allan Publishing 'Heritage Railway of the Year Award' in 2011, and there are plans to extend services a further 4 miles to Honeybourne, possibly by 2020, resulting in a total length of 19 miles.

GREAT CENTRAL RAILWAY

The original Great Central Railway dates back to 1897, with its 'London Extension' being completed two years later to allow direct journeys to the capital from Nottingham, Leicester, Sheffield and Manchester. As such it was the last steam main-line to be completed in the UK, but the plans of its Chairman, Sir Edward Watkin, to link his railway with France by way of a Channel Tunnel were ultimately thwarted, largely a result of the route being considered a duplicate of the Midland Main Line in Dr Beeching's report, and therefore earmarked for closure, which came into effect in 1966. It is hard to imagine how this ambitious brainchild of the great Edward Watkin could die

Left: Ex LMS 'Jubilee' Class 4-6-0 No (4)5593 *Kolhapur* stands at Quorn with a recreation of 'The Lakes Express', which actually ran in BR days from Euston to both Workington and Penrith via Keswick on the West Coast route. *Gary Thornton*

Below left: The replica *Rocket* is seen on tour in 2009 as it stands at Loughborough station. *Michael H. C. Baker*

Below: Class 'O4' 2-8-0 No 63601 is seen in a view taken from the overbridge at Loughborough station in 2009. *Michael H. C. Baker*

No 506 *Butler-Henderson* pauses at Rothley on 18 November 1989 whilst running round its train, before returning to Loughborough Central. The 'smudge' on the smokebox is from having '62660' – its BR number – adorned in chalk earlier in the day and since rubbed out! *John Stretton*

so soon, or how its heart would be massaged back to life in such an unlikely area. But beat again it did, just a flicker at first, but destined to grow stronger every day.

Just three years after closure, the Mainline Preservation Group (MLPG) was formed with the aim of restoring a section of the line as a double-track heritage railway. The Loughborough to Leicester section (which hadn't closed until 1969) was eventually chosen and work began to salvage materials and begin the process of restoration. The base for operations was Loughborough Central station, leased in 1970, to be followed the following year by the purchase of the rest of the railway, and by 1972 the first vehicles were arriving in Loughborough yard.

On 3 September 1973 LMS 'Black 5' No 5231 hauled the first passenger train on the new railway to Quorn and back. Further purchases of track involved share issues, and the Main Line Steam Trust (MLST) was formed to achieve the charitable status necessary to support the company's target of raising the large

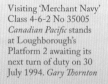

Visiting 'Merchant Navy' Class 4-6-2 No 35005 *Canadian Pacific* stands at Loughborough's Platform 2 awaiting its next turn of duty on 30 July 1994. *Gary Thornton*

Left: 'Deltic' D9019 *Royal Highland Fusilier* is seen at Leicester North on 30 July 1994 resplendent in the much-loved two-tone green livery of the early BR diesel years. She was to leave the following year to run on the East Lancashire Railway. *Gary Thornton*

sum of money needed to extend operations south towards Leicester, in what was described in 1976 as one of the most ambitious projects ever attempted, that of preserving a main line in a highly populated area. Nevertheless, by the following year nearly £1.25 million had been raised by voluntary means, a great achievement in the story of what was certainly the most expensive private railway in the UK.

Later, with the formation of what would become the Great Central Railway (Nottingham) Ltd, the first section of track south from Ruddington to East Leake was added. Thus the GCR became two adjacent sections: that in Leicestershire has 5½ miles of what is currently Britain's only double-track heritage main line, and runs for a total of 7¾ miles from Loughborough to a new terminus just north of Leicester, while the Nottinghamshire section, based at Ruddington, has a rail and road vehicle preservation site called the Nottingham Transport Heritage Centre, with track running southwards for 10 miles to the Midland Main Line at Loughborough. A major project for the future is to reinstate the bridges over the national network at Loughborough and thereby rejoin the two railways to form a combined length of 18 miles of double-track line.

In the early days, services were often worked by 'Black 5' No 5231, by now named *3rd (Volunteer) Battalion, The Worcestershire and Sherwood Foresters Regiment*, but by the 1980s the growing stock of LNER locos were more usually to be seen in action, such as 'N2' Class 0-6-2T No 4744 or Thompson 'B1' 4-6-0 No 1306 *Mayflower*, which would haul well-loaded trains through Leicestershire's finest scenic area, Charnwood. Indeed, the 1980s were already being hailed as 'the decade when the GCR becomes Great again'.

Today, the stock list for the GCR is impressive and features several locos that operate main-line charters or may be in demand as loans to other heritage lines. These include SR 'N15' 4-6-0 No 30777 *Sir Lamiel* and 'West Country' 4-6-2 No 34039 *Boscastle*; LMS 'Black 5s' Nos 45231 and 45305, 2MT No 46521, 3F No 47406 and 8F No 48305; GWR 4MT 2-6-2T No 4141 and 'Modified Hall' 4-6-0 No 6990 *Witherslack Hall*; LNER 2-8-0 No 63601 and 'N2' No 69523; and BR 'Britannia' Class 4-6-2 No

Below: Loughborough in 1972 – the early days! The Robinson '11F' 'Improved Director' Class 4-4-0s were new to the Great Central Railway in 1920, and No 506 *Butler-Henderson* was still in BR service in 1960, when it was withdrawn and saved as part of the National Collection. *Michael H. C. Baker*

70013 *Oliver Cromwell*, 5MT No 73156 and 2MT No 78019.

The diesel fleet includes 'Peak' No D123, 'Brush 4' No D1705, Class 25 No D5185, Class 31 No D5830 and Class 33 No D6535, as well as several other locomotives and DMUs.

Trains run every weekend of the year, on Bank Holidays and on certain weekdays in the summer, and the GCR boasts that it is 'the only place in the world where full-size steam engines can be seen regularly passing each other, just as it was when steam ruled the rails'.

Above and right: With No 45231 in the background, 'West Country' Class 4-6-2 No 34039 *Boscastle* is the centre of attention at Loughborough shed on 14 August 1994. *John Stretton*

LNER 'A4' Class 4-6-2 No 4498 (60007) *Sir Nigel Gresley* storms out of Loughborough Central on 28 December 1993 with the 1300 to Leicester North during the GCR's Christmas Gala. *John Stretton*

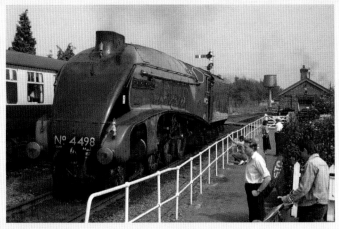

By 30 July 1994 the weather was considerably better and No 4498 is seen again coming off shed to resume her duties for the day. *Gary Thornton*

Representing the LMS large express locomotives, 'Duchess' Class 4-6-2 No 46229 *Duchess of Hamilton* arrives at Leicester North on 14 August 1994, with the 0930 from Loughborough Central. *John Stretton*

KEIGHLEY & WORTH VALLEY RAILWAY

The Keighley & Worth Valley Railway was bought from BR and reopened as a preserved line on 29 June 1968, at first operating a weekends and Bank Holidays service through the summer of that year using locos such as Ivatt 2-6-2T No 41241 and SR 'USA' 0-6-0T No 72. On that opening day, these two locomotives double-headed the first train from a Keighley platform decorated with bunting, while at Oxenhope they were met by a brass band playing 'Congratulations'. This was the first reopening to the public of a preserved standard-gauge branch line since the Bluebell Railway had been inaugurated in 1960.

The 5-mile stretch of formerly derelict line runs from Keighley to Oxenhope in West Yorkshire. Built by local mill-owners in 1867, then bought up by the rapidly expanding Midland Railway in 1881 and surviving until its closure as part of the railway cutbacks in 1962, the K&WVR is a complete branch line in its original form, set in the heart of the Pennines and winding its way through the industrial landscape of the old West Riding, beside mills with their tall chimneys, reminding us all of our heritage, born out of cotton, wool, coal and steam, running on steep gradients to the moorland towns of Haworth and Oxenhope at the head of the valley.

Keighley is the railway's main-line junction, on the Leeds-Carlisle route. In 1971 it was the only station shared by BR and a preserved railway, with the Worth Valley trains using Platform 4. Oxenhope is 320 feet higher than Keighley, so the trains are forced to climb continuously, with a stretch of 1 in 56 on leaving Keighley station, followed by long inclines at 1 in 60 and 1 in 68. The average gradient of the line is 1 in 70, so engines and crew must work hard and the effect within the confines of the valley is dramatic.

Visitors to Haworth during 1972 admire preserved ex-LMS 2-6-2T No 41241 and ex-BR Standard 2-6-4 tank No 80002.

A regular visitor to the railway in its formative years was Bishop Eric Treacy MBE, who became its President. One-time Rector of Keighley, later Archdeacon of Halifax, then in 1968 Bishop of Wakefield, he was one of the few Bishops ever to preach a sermon from the tender of a steam locomotive, or to have a locomotive named after him. Tragically he died on 13 May 1978, perhaps fittingly by the lineside of his beloved Settle & Carlisle line at Appleby, camera in hand, enjoying to the last his abiding love of so many years. Here he is seen chatting with a volunteer at Haworth during a visit in 1972.

After 1962 the line remained closed for six years, during which time local passengers and freight customers found alternative means of transport, but on reopening a weekend 'shopper' service and a daily steam-hauled service during the summer and at holiday times proved that the line was still viable, and the policy of providing a reliable service to the communities along the Worth Valley paid dividends, with passengers flocking back. Valuable publicity arrived in

'USA' 2-8-0 No 5820 undergoes a steam test at Haworth in November 1990.

the shape of BBC TV, which used the line in 1968 to film its Sunday serial *The Railway Children*, followed by the famous feature film.

Since 1968 the line has been owned, operated and managed entirely by volunteer members of the preservation society. There is no General Manager, no Board, no full-time staff. The branch was bought from British Railways on a zero-interest instalment plan that would take 25 years to complete at £3,500 per year, including everything except the last 100 yards into Keighley's No 4 platform, which was leased. At the time of its opening, the adult return fare from Keighley to Oxenhope was 4 shillings, with half price for children. The line's headquarters are at Haworth, where the engine sheds accommodate most of the collection of locomotives and provide a powerful attraction, bringing visitors to experience the thrill of the steam railway that now operates on almost 200

Ex-SR 'West Country' Class 'Pacific' No 34092 *City of Wells* stands resplendent outside the shed in August 1983.

days per year and combines perfectly with Haworth's other claim to fame – the Brontes. The town flourishes.

The loco stock in the early 1970s included an impressive collection of representatives from the pre-BR companies, as well as a good number of 'industrials'. From the LMS were 8F 2-8-0 No 48431, 'Black 5' Nos 45212 and 5025, 2-6-0 No 2700 and 2MT 2-6-2T No 41241, together with L&YR 0-6-0 No 957. The LNER was represented by 0-6-0T No 69023 *Joem*, when not on loan to the Derwent Valley Light Railway in York. The SR contributed 'West Country' Class 4-6-2 No 34092 *City of Wells* and 0-6-0T No 72, while from the GWR there was 0-6-0PT No 5775, the 'Old Gentleman's engine' from *The Railway Children*.

'Black 5' No 45212, sporting a 24F shedplate and home depot name 'Fleetwood' on her buffer beam, arrives at Haworth station with a train from Keighley, then blasts away towards Oxenhope a few minutes later.

Former Lancashire & Yorkshire Railway Class '25' 0-6-0 No 957 (BR Class 2F No 52044) is seen at Haworth in August 1981. Introduced in 1887 and withdrawn in 1959, she starred in *The Railway Children* as 'The Green Dragon'.

9F 2-10-0 No 92220 *Evening Star* eases her train out of Haworth towards Oxenhope during the summer of 1972.

All is quiet between trains at Haworth in August 1983 – but not for long...

...as 'USA' Class 'S160' 2-8-0 No 5820 brings in a train from Keighley. Built for the US Army Transportation Corps and shipped to Britain in large numbers during the Second World War for use during the invasion of France, these locos were employed by all four of Britain's main railway companies under the control of the War Department, hauling heavy freight trains, before being shipped to France. After the war they were disposed of to a number of European countries, which were rebuilding following the devastation. No 5820 is one of six 'S160s' re-imported to work on our preserved railways.

Haworth station has changed little over the years, apart from landscaping on the other side of the track from the platform. It attracts the most road-borne passengers and visitors of all the Worth Valley's stations, as its lattice footbridge offers an excellent vantage point to observe the arrivals and departures.

The tiny station at Ingrow West in January 1990, recently restored after years of neglect.

Ex-BR 4MT No 75078 arrives at Ingrow on the same day.

Top left: 4MT 4-6-0 No 75078 is seen near Damems, en route for Haworth from Keighley in January 1990. Damems is probably one of the smallest stations (not a 'halt') in the country, retaining a Station Master until 1947, and includes a level crossing and 1923-vintage crossing-keeper's house. To recreate the facilities of the original station, a signal box and booking office have also been transplanted from Earby and Keighley respectively.

Top right: Also seen in January 1990, the lovingly restored station at Oakworth, which was the setting for the film *The Railway Children*, retains its gas lighting and regularly appears among the winners of the ARPS/Ian Allan 'Best Restored Station' competition.

Above: On steam gala days, not every train stops at Oakworth, so would-be passengers must stand back to appreciate the power of steam passing at speed as 'Dub D' 2-8-0 No 90733 races through towards Haworth.

'Black 5' No 45212 passes the derelict remains of Keighley's signal box during 1972. The box was dispensed with by BR in 1956, as a reduction in train services on this single-track branch line no longer warranted its use, and of course the branch was closed altogether in 1962.

9F No 92220 *Evening Star* pulls into Keighley in 1972.

In January 1990 at Keighley station, ex-BR 4MT No 75078 prepares to take her train along the Worth Valley to Oxenhope. Platform 4 has been restored to the London Midland Region style of the 1950s (even though this was once North Eastern Region territory); the ticket office was once a sweet kiosk at Manchester Central station, and the buffet and departure clock are L&YR in origin.

The line from Carnforth, northwards along Morecambe Bay, then across Arnside Viaduct to skirt the southern Lake District by way of Ulverston to Barrow-in-Furness, then northwards again along the coast to Whitehaven, was the domain of the Furness Railway Company. Its original two sections of railway of 1846, each of just over 6 miles, had been extended steadily by the time of its absorption into the LMS at the 1923 'Grouping'. It had prospered during the 1850s

This Furness Railway 'Caution to Trespassers' notice near Ulverston, dated 1894 and photographed in 1974, warns of a fine of up to 'Forty Shillings' (about £1,000 today) for any such offence.

LMS 'Black 5' No 44806 approaches Newby Bridge with a train from Lakeside during the early days of the L&HR in 1973. She was adopted by Thames Television's *Magpie* programme on 1 August of that year, and named *Magpie* by Susan Stranks, one of the programme's presenters.

John Townsend

and 1860s by bringing coal and iron ore from the rich deposits in the Furness area (then part of Lancashire) and from the Cumberland coast, for use in the heavy industries of Lancashire and Yorkshire. Access to Barrow-in-Furness was also vital, as with the new railway came a transformation from an insignificant fishing community to a highly industrialised

0-4-0ST No 1 *Caliban*, dating from 1937, shunts in the yard at Haverthwaite during 1974.

The now entirely functional station at Lakeside is alongside the quay to allow easy transfer to the steamers. During the eight years between the closure of the branch and its reopening, the classic Edwardian station buildings were demolished, a fate later suffered by the overall roof, which had been declared unsafe by the British Rail Property Board in 1978. Here 0-6-0ST No 14 *Princess*, built in 1942, has brought in a train from Haverthwaite, for passengers to enjoy the next stage of their journey – after thanking the engine's crew, of course.

town, with spacious docks, shipbuilding and armaments works, steelworks, timber yards, sawmills and much more. At the same time, and quick to realise the potential for tourist traffic, the Furness Railway sought to expand further into the southern Lake District. As early as 1847 the Kendal & Windermere Railway Company had opened a branch line from Oxenholme on the new Lancaster & Carlisle Railway, to Birthwaite, a tiny village on the lake, which, with the arrival of the railway, was renamed Windermere.

Today, the old Furness line, with gradients in places steeper than its more famous northern neighbour, the Settle & Carlisle, with lovely coastal stretches, and combining as it does the beauty of river and mountain scenery, is probably unequalled anywhere else in England. Sadly, only three locomotives from the Furness Railway are preserved: 0-4-0 No 3 *Coppernob*, dating from 1846 and now housed in the National Railway Museum, 0-4-0ST No 18 *Chloe*, of 1863 vintage, which spent more than 40 years working at Barrow Steelworks but now graces the L&HR, and 0-4-0ST No 25, later renumbered 6 and housed at Steamtown, Carnforth, also a survivor from Barrow Steelworks.

The Furness branch from Plumpton Junction near Ulverston, along the estuary of the River Leven, through Greenodd to Haverthwaite and onwards through Newby Bridge to Lakeside on Windermere, was begun in 1867. It proved a short but difficult project, with the hard rock around Haverthwaite being particularly resistant to cutting and tunnelling. Opened behind schedule in 1869, the less than 8 miles soon became a busy freight line, carrying coal for the Windermere steamers, iron ore for the Backbarrow Iron Works and sulphur and saltpetre for the Black Beck and Low Wood gunpowder works, which were among five operating in southern Lakeland, eventually to be absorbed into the ICI Group in the early 1970s. The siting of gunpowder factories here was a result of the protection offered by well-timbered valleys (which also provided the materials for producing charcoal as well as the wood for gunpowder barrels), the sparsely populated countryside and the abundant water power available. Before the coming of the railway, the raw materials were brought in via the port of Greenodd near Ulverston, then by boat up the River Leven, with the finished products travelling in the opposite direction. The completion of the railway line up the Leven Valley to Newby Bridge and Lakeside opened up the opportunity for both Black Beck and Low Wood gunpowder works to make use of the new facility, and both companies constructed their own tramways to connect into the new rail outlet. Horses were used to haul the wagons on these tramways – no locomotives being allowed into the works for obvious reasons – and even the horses were copper-shod. It is also likely that the rails on the sites were of non-ferrous metals. Back down the line came pig iron, gunpowder, pit props and livestock.

As the iron ore industry fell into decline during the 1870s, the railway would have followed, had it not been associated with the steamer traffic on the lake from its earliest days, providing an important link in the tourist route for those eager to explore the wonderful scenery of the Lake District. Passenger traffic became the line's mainstay, with trainloads of day-trippers and holidaymakers seeking to escape the grime of the mill towns of industrial Lancashire. The normal locos in use were the Furness 4-4-2Ts, built for use on both the Lakeside and Coniston branches, later to give way to L&YR tank engines hauling LNWR carriages.

The advent of war followed by the increasing popularity of the motor car led to a gradual falling off of traffic, though the goods yard at Haverthwaite did continue to cater for local freight. Passenger numbers did recover for a time, becoming quite high during the summer months, but in winter usage was very light and it came as no surprise when the line was eventually closed to passenger traffic, as the 'Beeching Axe' fell on 6 September 1965. A thrice-weekly pick-up goods service continued to run to Haverthwaite and Backbarrow Iron Works until April 1967, when the ironworks finally ceased production and the route was closed to traffic altogether.

Plans to preserve and reopen the line were already under way, however. After the formation of the Lakeside Railway Estates Co Ltd in 1967, the acquisition two years later of the former BR motive power depot at Carnforth was part of a plan to create a live museum there, to be named Steamtown, where the locomotives would be housed, and the Lakeside Railway, which would operate them along the branch from the BR line at Plumpton Junction near Ulverston. Unfortunately, in 1968 BR decreed that it would not allow privately operated trains into its Ulverston station, and, equally dismaying, the Lake District Planning Board made it known that it wished to use a large part of Haverthwaite station yard and sections of the trackbed for improvements to the A590 trunk road. This was a disaster for the plans of the Lakeside Railway Estates Company. The upshot was the splitting of the project, to form the Steamtown Railway

The Furness Railway Trust-owned Hunslet-built Austerity 0-6-0ST *Cumbria* awaits departure from Haverthwaite in the summer of 2002 – evidenced by the shorts! *Cumbria* is painted in the livery of the Furness Railway, applied in 1995 to celebrate the 150th Anniversary of that railway company. In the second picture *Cumbria* is under way heading towards Lakeside. *Carol King/John Townsend*

Museum as a separate entity from the 3½ miles of track between Lakeside and Haverthwaite, which would be operated by a new company formed in 1970 and called the Lakeside & Haverthwaite Railway Co Ltd. In the same year, the BR Property Board approved the closure and impending sale of the branch line, and granted the new L&HR access for the purpose of moving stock purchased from BR at York, together with the available locomotives from storage at Carnforth, onto its intended section. These movements had to be completed with all haste, even though negotiations for the purchase of the available line had not been completed and a Light Railway Order had yet to be applied for, as without further ado in 1971 BR lifted the remainder of the track between Plumpton Junction and Haverthwaite, thereby cutting off this short railway from the rest of the railway network.

After further prolonged negotiations and the threat of a public enquiry precipitated by a single objection (later withdrawn) from a member of the public to the granting of the Light Railway Order, the issue was finally resolved in early 1973. Shortly afterwards, following a successful examination by the Railway Inspectorate, clearance was given to reopen the line for passenger traffic. So, in May 1973 the Lakeside & Haverthwaite Railway at last opened for business, after volunteers had been trained on the Keighley & Worth Valley line, thus reviving a century-old connection with the Windermere steamers at Lakeside station. The opening ceremony was performed by Britain's best-known railway photographer, the Right Reverend Eric Treacy LLD, Bishop of Wakefield, who travelled aboard the inaugural train and stopped at Newby Bridge Halt to plant a copper beech tree to commemorate 'the beginning of a new life'. The newly reopened section follows the course of the River Leven – Windermere's outflow – for all its length, passing through meadows, woodland, rock cuttings and a tunnel – in short, offering beautiful views of the stunning Lakeland scenery.

The headquarters are at Haverthwaite, an ideal choice for the southern terminus of the line, having a spacious goods yard and excellent access by way of the 'improved' A590 trunk road. Here also is the steam stock housed, which in the early 1970s included 'Black 5' No 44806, a pair of BR Class 4MT 2-6-4Ts, Nos 42073 and 42085 of Fairburn design introduced in 1945, which incidentally hauled that first special train, together with a small collection of 0-4-0 and 0-6-0 ex-industrial saddle tank locos.

The climb out of the station, at a gradient of 1 in 78, gets the journey off to a testing start. At the other end of the line, Lakeside station offers quayside transfer to the Windermere steamers and thereby extends the journey in an unusual and spectacular fashion. The station here once boasted three platforms, a large office block and clock tower, engine and carriage sheds, a water tower and a turntable. Sadly, most of this is long gone.

The pleasure craft now plying Windermere comprise four modern motor ships, of which *Swan*, *Swift* and *Tern* are reconstructions of the former FR's graceful steam yachts that bore those names. *Teal*, seen here approaching Lakeside, is a new addition, while alas the original fourth vessel, *Cygnet*, is no more.

Originally opened in 1862 as the Ruabon to Llangollen line, later extended to Corwen in 1865, the line was closed to passengers as part of the Beeching cuts in 1965. Part of the route was reopened as the narrow-gauge Bala Lake Railway in the early 1970s, and the Flint & Deeside Preservation Society was founded in 1972 with the aim of preserving a standard-gauge stretch of the line. Eventually focussing its attention on the Llangollen to Corwen section, the local council granted a lease to the society of Llangollen railway station building and 3 miles of track, in the hope that restoration would benefit the local economy by bringing more tourists into the area. The station was duly opened on 13 September 1975, with just 60 feet (18.3 metres) of track!

Two years later, Shell Oil donated a mile of unused track and this was laid over the ensuing four years using volunteer labour. Further donations extended the running track to 1¾ miles by 1986, and by 1996 the line had reached Carrog, a distance of 7½ miles, with plans to extend further to Corwen in the near future, where a new station would be built.

Locomotives in the early years consisted of GWR '5700' Class 0-6-0PT No 7754, built in 1930, and a handful of industrial locos and diesel shunters. Rolling stock in 1981 consisted of three coaches, two GWR brake vans, one SR parcels van, one LNER parcels van, four wagons, two tank wagons and a GWR steam crane, in working condition.

Left: The delightful setting of Llangollen station is apparent as an unidentified ex-GWR 'Prairie' tank locomotive awaits the signalman's decision to lower the home signal on 21 April 2007. *Peter Townsend*

Below: A popular feature on many preserved lines, particularly during gala weekends, is the running of demonstration goods trains in between the passenger turns. Here we see from a distance just such a train passing through Berwyn station during the 2007 spring gala. *Peter Rowlands*

We are now on board the demonstration freight seen in the previous photo waiting for an auto-train hauled by ex-GWR '6400' Class pannier tank No 6430 to clear the section.
Peter Townsend

The success of the railway has attracted the interest of many private companies and the associated funding has allowed the operation's steam loco stock to be greatly increased. Recently it has included: GWR 'Manor' Class 4-6-0 No 7822 *Foxcote Manor*, 2-8-0 No 3802, 0-6-2T No 5643 and 0-6-0PT No 6430, LMS 'Black 5' 4-6-0 No 44806 and 0-6-0T 'Jinty' No 7298, and BR Standard 2-6-4T No 80072. Several other GWR locos are under overhaul/restoration. The society also operates diesel locos: Class 26/0 No 26010, Class '37/0' No 37240 and Class '47/4' No 47449.

The railway runs alongside the beautiful River Dee, operating its predominantly steam-hauled trains throughout the year. With testing gradients set against the backdrop of the Welsh Mountains and calling at delightful and lovingly restored rural stations, the route succeeds in creating an authentic 1950s branch-line atmosphere, a tribute to the largely volunteer workforce.

A busy scene at Llangollen as 'Battle of Britain' Class 4-6-2 No 34081 *92 Squadron* and '5600' Class 0-6-2T No 5643 load and unload their respective trains.
Peter Townsend

MID HANTS RAILWAY

The Mid Hants Railway – the 'Watercress Line' – had become part of the London & South Western Railway in 1884, having arrived in the valley of the clear waters of the River Arle in 1865. The river provided perfect growing conditions for the locally grown 'superfood crop' – watercress – and the newly constructed railway allowed the fast distribution of the delicacy to Waterloo and Covent Garden Market by next morning. Thus watercress became big business.

A tranquil scene at Medstead & Four Marks station, as the train for Alresford awaits its signal.

The line was also an important alternative route between London and Southampton, particularly for military traffic between the army town of Aldershot and the embarkation port of Southampton. It became part of the Southern Railway in 1923, then the Southern Region of British Railways in 1948. It survived the 'Beeching Axe' in 1967, but was eventually closed by British Railways in 1973, when the last train ran over the Mid Hants route from Alton to Winchester on 4 February, marking the end of a protracted battle to save the trains that served this attractive and growing part of Hampshire.

Coming late onto the preservation scene meant a tough fight for the Mid Hants Railway Preservation Society. Hindered by its own changing objectives,

'West Country' Class No 34016 *Bodmin* waits for 'WD' 8F No 90775 to bring her train into Alresford, before departing towards Alton in April 1987.

BR Standard 4MT No 76017 simmers gently at Alresford.

raising the substantial capital required to launch an operational steam railway proved a tough task. First efforts at preservation envisaged securing the whole 17-mile line, but when this failed the Winchester & Alton Railway Limited opted for the much more limited but far more realistic goal of reintroducing steam-hauled trains over just 3 miles of line between Alresford and Ropley. This it achieved on 30 April 1977.

Although BR had lifted the track beyond Ropley and thereby left the preserved stretch of railway with no connection to the main line, the company had been farsighted enough to purchase all the land and buildings between Alresford and Alton in anticipation of one day being able to re-lay the line over Medstead Bank, giving a total run of 10 miles.

By 1981 plans by the Winchester & Alton Railway, now supported by its largest shareholder, the Mid Hants Railway Preservation Society, were well advanced for the extension to Alton, so much so that during October of the previous year BR had offered the opportunity to allow the eventual use of Platform 3 by the society, from Easter 1984 if work went according to plan.

By 1982 reports had been commissioned that confirmed that the trackbed that would carry the extension towards Alton was still in a serviceable condition, and gangs of volunteers were marshalled to begin undergrowth clearance and other preparatory work, prior to ballast renewal and finally track-laying. During that year, the first 3 miles from Ropley to Medstead & Four Marks made steady progress at the rate of about 200 yards per week, though actual track-laying was confined to weekends, with the necessary 'prep' being carried out during the week.

'West Country' Class No 34016 *Bodmin* prepares to take her train away from Alresford, with plenty of steam to spare.

Plans at this stage were to operate the first public services to Medstead & Four Marks in the form of 'Santa Specials' during the winter of 1982/83 and to reach the BR station at Alton by Easter 1984. This was always viewed as one of the most ambitious schemes being undertaken in the railway preservation movement, but on 25 May 1985 the long-sought goal of connection to the Southern Region of BR at Alton was finally achieved. The potential for increased business that this 'plug-in' could generate would be enormous, and to help ensure smooth operations within the station some sidings and a 'run-round' facility were essential additions to the scheme.

On 24 July 1985 the seal of approval was at last placed on the endeavours of the Mid Hants Railway by the official opening of the section from Ropley to

Alton. Even though the line had to be closed on that day so that it could be officially 'opened', the disappointed visitors who had arrived, presumably having not seen the posters and leaflets detailing such matters, were eventually rewarded with a free train ride. The special train on that day was hauled by rebuilt Bulleid 'West Country' 'Pacific' No 34016 *Bodmin*, from Alresford to Ropley, where a tape across the line was ceremoniously cut before the train continued to Alton. The newly completed run-round loop flanking Platform 3 allowed the two waiting former Southern Railway 2-6-0 locos, 'N' Class No 31874 *Brian Fisk* and 'U' Class No 31806, coupled tender to tender, to haul the train back towards Alresford. The line could be said to be well and truly open at last, with signalling installed and new signal boxes operational at Alresford and Medstead & Four Marks, though much was still needed to be done, including the furnishing and equipping of the box at Alton. However, the station there has been completely repainted in the cream and green style of the Southern Railway, and with the through ticketing arrangements with BR Southern Region a welcome spirit of cooperation is evident in the joint working at the station. A similar SR paint scheme has been applied to Medstead & Four Marks and Alresford stations, while the colours of the London & South Western Railway have been used at Ropley.

Fellow SR survivors: 'N' Class No 31874, now named *Brian Fisk*, has been receiving attention at Ropley.

The section of line between the market towns of Alresford to Alton, now marketed as the 'Watercress Line', thus runs for 10 steeply graded miles, and preserves an important piece of our railway heritage. The effort required of men and machines to crest the notorious summit at the highest station above sea level in southern England, Medstead and Four Marks, led crews in steam days to nickname the feat as 'going over the Alps', but perseverance has prevailed and now the line is a thriving concern.

The steam locomotive stock in the early 1980s was impressive, and it needed to be to tackle the steep gradients of 1 in 60 at Medstead Bank. It included a pair of ex-LSWR 'S15s', Nos 30499 and 506, of 1920 vintage, three SR 2-6-0s, Nos 31625, 31806 and 31874, and no fewer than four SR 'Pacifics', 'West Country' Class Nos 34016 *Bodmin* and 34105 *Swanage*, 'Battle of Britain' Class No 34067 *Tangmere*, and 'Merchant Navy' Class No 35018 *British India Line*. Added to these were ex-LMS 4F No 44123 and 3F No 47324, BR 4MT No 76017 and a handful of 0-4-0 and 0-6-0 saddle tank 'industrials'.

Behind the 'N' is Class 'T9' 4-4-0 No 30120, a Drummond-designed loco for the LSWR, introduced in 1899.

Above: 'WD' 8F 2-10-0 No 90775, one of the few surviving 'Dub Ds', a class that once numbered more than 750 locos, takes her train away from Alton in April 1987.

Top right: Later the same day No 90775 is seen leaving Alresford.

Above right: Receiving attention in April 1987 is BR Class 4MT No 76017, now named *Hermes.*

Right: Back in steam again, No 76017 approaches Alresford, her fireman ready to give up the single-line token on 8 August 1991.

Far left: Lunch is served: a young volunteer waits at Alresford station with a tray for the crew.

Left: The driver and fireman of No 76017 look back in anticipation of the signal to run round their train at Alresford station on 8 August 1991.

Mid-Norfolk Railway

The Mid-Norfolk Railway opened as a heritage railway as late as 1997, running through the centre of Norfolk between the market towns of Wymondham and Dereham, via Yaxham, Thuxton and Kimberley Park, a distance of 11½ miles.

The line was originally opened between 1847 and 1857 and became part of the Great Eastern Railway in 1862. It was important as a passenger and freight

Dereham station looks 'brand new' in this view taken on 6 March 2009. This represents the excellent results achieved by hard work and enthusiasm, the building having been restored following a serious fire that had gutted it.

route, being especially heavily used during the war years for the transport of materials used at local airfields, and at other times for the movement of agricultural products, for example during the sugar beet season.

The gradual closing of sections to passenger services occurred between 1952 and 1969, although goods traffic continued until final closure took place in June 1989. Following unsuccessful attempts to preserve sections of the line, a new company, Great Eastern Railway (1989) Ltd, was formed to save it, but problems continued until in 1995 the Mid Norfolk Railway Preservation Trust was established through the merger of campaign groups and organisations involved in trying to re-establish passenger services. By April 1998 the Trust had completed the purchase of the route between Wymondham and Dereham, with the original Dereham station being reopened to passengers on Saturday 26 July 1997 using motive power in the form of 1890-built Manning-Wardle 0-6-0T *Sir Berkeley*, hired from the Keighley & Worth Valley Railway. Commercial freight trains were re-established the following year and the full passenger service commenced in 1999.

The railway has a connection with the national rail network at Wymondham, allowing access for both freight and passenger charters and excursions. The Mid-Norfolk Railway owns a large collection of heritage rolling stock, and although trains are mostly diesel-operated, steam locos are sometimes used on timetabled trains, most often in the form of GWR '9400' Class 0-6-0PT No 9466, a 4F taper-boiler design by Hawksworth, introduced in 1947 originally for heavy shunting duties. Guest steam locomotives make regular appearances during the summer months.

Further evidence of the progress being made at the MNR, with restored level crossing gates, signals, water tower and immaculate Class 47 No 47850 *County of Essex*. *Gary Thornton*

Railway Pubs and Signs

Above: The love of railways and in particular the steam age is forever marked in the number of public houses that proudly display their heritage for all to see in the signs outside the premises. Though sadly no more due to rebranding and renaming, the 'Railway King' in York was appropriately located in George Hudson Street. The pub sign depicts a scene inside York railway station. Not far away, 'The Leeman' remembers another former Lord Mayor and Hudson's political opponent, George Leeman. Around the corner, the 'Jubilee' celebrates our railway heritage more directly.

Below: It is not too difficult to find more signs reminding us of the railway legacy in the York area.

NATIONAL RAILWAY MUSEUM, YORK

On an elevated section of original track beside the museum entrance, a Stockton & Darlington 'cauldron' wagon offers a taste of the railway history to be found within.

In the 1970s a change of teaching post allowed me to return to the North of England, to the beautiful and historic city of York, with its own strong railway tradition dating back to the 1830s. That was the era of the York & North Midland Railway, and its architect, the 'Railway King' and three times Lord Mayor, George Hudson. In York one is never far from a railway line, and the 'Carriage Works' was a major employer in the city for generations. The love of railways, and in particular the steam age, is also forever remembered in a number of public houses, which proudly display their heritage for all to see in the signs outside the premises.

In addition to being an important railway centre in its own right, York is ideally located to allow easy access to the preserved railways starting to thrive in the Yorkshire moors and dales. Although 'Rail 150' at Shildon was unquestionably the 'big event' of the year, 1975 also saw the National Collection of preserved steam locomotives, assembled in the lovingly refurbished old steam shed at York, unveiled on 27 September, when the National Railway Museum was officially opened by HRH Prince Philip, Duke of Edinburgh. The NRM is the largest railway museum in the world, responsible for the conservation and interpretation of the British National Collection of historically significant railway vehicles and other artefacts.

Built around the two turntables of the former York engine shed, the Main Hall houses a wide variety of locomotives, rolling stock and rescued relics of all kinds from the steam era up to the present day, including one locomotive, SR 'Merchant Navy' 'Pacific' No 35029 *Ellerman Lines*, sectioned to show its internal workings.

A sectioned locomotive, SR 'Merchant Navy' 'Pacific' No 35029 *Ellerman Lines*, shows its internal workings.

In October 1975 visitors flock to examine the locomotives around one of the NRM's two turntables. In the background are Nos 92220 *Evening Star*, 4468 *Mallard* and 4771 *Green Arrow*, with Midland 'Compound' No 1000 in the foreground.

The first turntable, at the north end of the Hall, has 24 tracks available for the locomotives, with some of the pits under these tracks having been modernised and fitted with side lighting so that visitors can walk beneath the locos and clearly see the working mechanism between the frames.

Locomotives on display in 1975 included: GNR Stirling 'Single' 4-2-2 No 1; NER 2-4-2 No 66 *Aerolite*; SR 4-6-2 No 35029 *Ellerman Lines* (sectioned); Furness 0-4-0 No 3 *Coppernob*; Shutt End Railway 0-4-0 *Agenoria*; LB&SCR 'Terrier' 0-6-0ST No 82 *Boxhill*; GER 0-6-0T No 87; NER Bo-Bo electric No 1; GWR 2-8-0 No 2818; GNR 4-4-2 No 990 *Henry Oakley*; GNR 4-4-2 No 251; LNWR 2-4-0 No 790 *Hardwicke*; GER 2-4-0 No 490; BR 2-10-0 No 92220 *Evening Star*; SE&CR Wainwright 4-4-0 No 737; LNER 'A4' 4-6-2 No 4468 *Mallard*; LSWR Adams 4-4-0 No 563; MR 'Compound' 4-4-0 No 1000; Grand Junction Railway 2-2-2 No 49 *Columbine*; LB&SCR 0-4-2 No 214 *Gladstone*; and NER 4-4-0 No 1621.

Other locomotives have taken their place around the turntable over time, often being housed here between duties on the increasingly popular steam specials.

On a quieter day, NER 4-4-0 No 1621 (right) stands alongside No 35029 *Ellerman Lines*.

The museum's second turntable is home to a fine collection of carriages, seen here during October 1975.

Part of the museum's collection of rolling stock is arranged around the second turntable, and this includes LNWR Royal Saloons for King Edward VII and Queen Victoria, together with LNWR Royal Dining Car No 76, as well as a Post Office Sorting Van, Pullman Car 'Topaz', the Duke of Sutherland's Saloon, replicas of Liverpool & Manchester coaches, and examples of early stock from pre-'Grouping' days.

A viewing balcony runs the full length of the Main Hall, from which the entire display can be appreciated, and nearby is a refreshment room with a view of the East Coast Main Line, which runs alongside the museum.

It was perhaps inevitable that at least in its early days the museum's collection of locomotives would reflect its NER/LNER origins, while the carriage collection has a strong LNWR/LMS element.

The bulk of the GWR collection is housed at Swindon, while most of the purely Scottish items are located in the Glasgow Museum. Added to this, a vast number and variety of items have been successfully preserved and restored by private groups throughout Britain.

The museum was an instant success. Entry was free and 170,000 visitors flocked through the doors in the first three weeks. Car parking became a nightmare as every car park in York was filled. Traffic chaos in the city was blamed on the influx of so many visitors, and a police spokesman was quoted in the local paper, the *Evening Press*, as saying, 'We don't know the answer to it. We have nowhere left to send the cars.'

The full-length balcony affords excellent views of the exhibits arranged around the turntables.

Original estimates by museum officials were that 700,000 people would visit the museum in the first year, but the number had reached 500,000 by the end of November, just two months after opening. The total rose to 1 million on 22 April 1976, with 2 million being recorded in less than a year. Dr John Coiley, Keeper of the NRM, said, 'I don't like to be proved wrong in public, but this time I am delighted to have been in the wrong.'

Of course, the National Collection of railway locomotives, rolling stock and associated items is far larger than could ever be displayed within one museum, even one as spacious as the NRM with its 2-acre Main Hall; in 1978 it consisted of more than 80 locomotives and well over 100 items of rolling stock, having inherited more than 90% of the collection from the closed Museum of British Transport in Clapham, south London, together with all of

that from the old York Queen Street museum. Given its commitment to its primary obligation of preserving significant items from the history of railways as they affected Britain, it is inevitable that the collection will continue to grow.

It was seen as vital from the start that the new NRM should be outgoing and an integral part of the railway preservation movement as a whole – to extend the museum beyond a display of static exhibits. The goodwill gained by its participation in the 'Rail 150' celebrations at Shildon, particularly in sending NER 2-4-0 No 910 virtually at the last moment and at a particularly hectic time for NRM staff, did much to lay the foundations for the policy of loaning locos to preserved lines and the reciprocal exhibition of privately restored engines.

A model recalling the early days of the railways stands in the Main Hall. Loaded trucks from mines or quarries trundled downhill under gravity to be unloaded, then the 'empties' were dragged back up again by horses, which would travel back down again with the next load.

A further measure of the York museum's success is that when its predecessor, the Museum of British Transport in Clapham, closed in 1973, nearly 1¾ million visitors had passed through its turnstiles, while between its opening in 1975 and October 1977 3¼ million people had visited the NRM, and there had been occasions when York's attendances outstripped even those at the Science Museum in South Kensington.

The importance of the NRM as a centre for education was stressed by the first Keeper of the Museum, Dr John Coiley. With this in mind, an education officer was appointed and a lecture room with projection facilities was provided on the premises. Another important part of the museum is the library, which contains printed material, photographs and engineering drawings initially inherited from Clapham but rapidly supplemented from the Public Record Office in London (mainly timetables), together with other purchases, donations and bequests, so that by 1982 the collection numbered around 12,000 volumes, including journals, accident reports, maps and junction diagrams, as well as a very large collection of locomotive test data relating mainly to steam traction.

Added to this came a collection from British Rail of nearly 100,000 photographic negatives, mainly glass plates dating from 1866, detailing the appearance of new locomotives as well as recording the day-to-day scenes from the works at Derby, Horwich and Crewe. To supplement these official records, the museum has also acquired several large and notable private collections of railway negatives over the years, and this policy of acquisition will continue to be

Also on display is part of the collection of headboards…

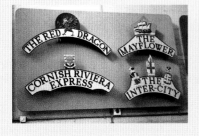

...together with a considerable variety of signs and notices...

actively pursued, as will be the programme of printing material and producing reference albums for the benefit of library readers and the wider community of railway enthusiasts.

The collection of mechanical engineering drawings held by the NRM will

probably total as many as 250,000 items, covering the total period of railway development, with both general arrangement drawings of locos and vast numbers showing components and details from a time when photography was not yet developed enough for such purposes. Though detailed cataloguing had not been completed by the early 1980s, it was hoped that further copies of some drawings would be made available for use by preservation groups as well as for inspection in the library.

By the 1980s the NRM was being increasingly used as a 'stabling point' for locomotives involved in steam charter tours, and visitors could see at close hand the arrivals and departures as they occurred on the adjacent BR sidings.

In recent years the museum has been extended to accommodate the former Goods Depot, so forming the new Station Hall, with platforms of sufficient length to allow locomotives and their carriages to be displayed together, and featuring a pleasant coffee shop and cafe between the platforms. This development effectively doubled the size of the museum and was instrumental in its gaining the 'Museum of the Year Award' in 1990.

...and several locomotive nameplates, those shown here being from locomotives of the 'Royal Scot', 'Jubilee', 'Princess' and 'Coronation' Classes of the LMS.

In 1999, 'The Works' was opened to allow visitors to view restoration projects from a gallery and provide access to a far greater proportion of the museum's vast collection. This in turn helped win the 'European Museum of the Year Award' in 2001. Since then, the Yorkshire Rail Academy was opened in 2004, a joint

LMS 'Coronation' Class 'Pacific' No 46229 *Duchess of Hamilton* takes a well-earned breather outside the museum on 2 July 1981.

LMS 'Black 5' No 5407 is shunted into the sidings, together with a rake of assorted vintage wagons, on 21 August 1981.

venture between the NRM and York College forming a purpose-built training centre and base for the museum's education teams.

Later in the same year, 'Locomotion – the NRM at Shildon, County Durham' was opened to the public, allowing still more of the NRM's collection to be displayed in that most appropriate setting, the birthplace of the modern railway.

The latest venture for the museum is 'Search Engine', a vast archive and research centre that allows visitors to

Above: In July 1984 two very different locos were welcomed into the turntable area of the Main Hall. One was the working replica of Stephenson's famous *Rocket*, winner of the Rainhill Trials of 1829.

Above right: The other was 'Deltic' No 55002 (D9002) *The King's Own Yorkshire Light Infantry*, built in 1961 and restored and preserved at the NRM.

Right: In 'The Works', Gresley-designed Class 'V2' No 4771 *Green Arrow* (BR number 60800) is undergoing further repairs on 26 October 2006.

view previously unseen documents, maps, photographs and small artefacts for research purposes or simply out of general interest.

All this has made the NRM one of the most popular museums in Great Britain, perhaps even in the world, and plans are being developed to allow access to still more displays in the future, to further reveal the massive impact the railways have had in shaping our modern world.

Above: On 22 October 1984 visitors could see preserved BR 0-6-0 diesel shunter No 03073 (D2073), built at Doncaster in 1959, and preserved NER 25-ton steam breakdown crane No DE 331153, built by Cravens Railway Carriage & Wagon Company in 1907.

Left: Having been retired from hauling steam charters in the late 1960s due to cracked frames and other problems following her withdrawal by BR in 1966, during July 1988 'A4' 'Pacific' *Bittern* (LNER number 4464, BR number 60019) was on show at the museum after being cosmetically restored as long-gone sister loco No 2509 *Silver Link*. No 2509 had been built in 1935 to pull the new 'Silver Jubilee' express service between London King's Cross and Newcastle, inaugurated to commemorate the Silver Jubilee of King George V. The train was painted silver throughout and ran until the outbreak of the Second World War in 1939. No 2509 was withdrawn from service in 1963 when East Coast Main Line express services were taken over by 'Deltic' diesel locos. She was not preserved and was broken up at Darlington Works. Sister loco *Bittern* would later be fully restored and returned to service pulling steam specials.

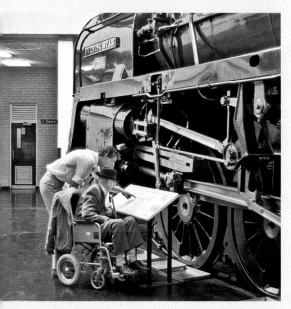

Checking her over: BR Standard Class 9F 2-10-0 No 92220 *Evening Star*, built at Swindon Works in 1960, was the last steam locomotive built by British Railways and is unique in that it is the only British main-line steam loco earmarked for preservation from the date of construction. *Evening Star* was withdrawn in 1965 after only five years in service, and preserved as part of the National Collection. She was photographed in July 1988.

NENE VALLEY RAILWAY

Sporting smoke deflectors, Swedish 'B' Class 4-6-0 No 101 takes her train of continental rolling stock out of Wansford station across the River Nene during August 1984.

The Nene Valley Railway in Cambridgeshire runs between Peterborough Nene Valley and Yarwell Junction, a distance of 7½ miles, and includes three stops on the way at Orton Mere, Ferry Meadows and Wansford. Originally part of the London & Birmingham Railway, which brought the line to Peterborough in 1845, it was absorbed into the London & North Western Railway and became part of an important link between Eastern England and the Midlands, with trains from Peterborough to Rugby and to Northampton running along the valley; at the 'Grouping' of 1923 the line was incorporated into the LMS.

Following a steady decline in passenger numbers, the Peterborough-Northampton services ceased in 1964, followed by the Rugby services two years later. There was no great surprise, therefore, when it fell to the infamous 'Beeching Axe', being one of the last of his line closures in the mid-1960s, although it did survive as a freight-only line until 1972, when 127 years of railway history were brought to an end.

The Peterborough Railway Society was formed in 1971 from the Peterborough Locomotive Society, itself originally a local branch of the East Anglia Locomotive Preservation Society, formed with the aim of raising funds for the purchase and restoration of BR 'Pacific' No 70000 *Britannia*. This represented a unique partnership between a volunteer enthusiasts' society and a 'New Town' Corporation, in that by 1971 Peterborough was already embarked on a vast expansion programme, overseen by the Peterborough New Town Development Corporation. The announcement of the closure of the National Transport Museum at Clapham provided the spark that brought the railway society and the Development Corporation together, and although their scheme for a new museum to house the National Collection, together with a plan to create a steam train service over the remains of the former LNWR Nene Valley branch to Northampton and Market Harborough (from which BR was about to withdraw its freight services) was rejected by the Government, a second option presented in 1972 met with a more favourable response.

Peterborough Development Corporation took up the society's proposals for the 'Nene Valley Railway' – to run over the 5 miles from Longueville

On static display near the entrance to the railway, and photographed in August 1984, German DB '64' Class 2-6-2T No 64305 reminds visitors of the cosmopolitan nature of the NVR.

Junction on the western outskirts of the city to Wansford station on the A1, and agreed to buy the line and lease it to the society. Safeguarded by this agreement, the society could embark upon an ambitious campaign to obtain the necessary rolling stock and equipment, in order to run its preserved BR 'Standard 5' 4-6-0 No 73050; this had been bought for its scrap value in 1968 by the Rev Richard Paten, and intended as a static exhibit to be sited outside Peterborough Technical College as a monument to Peterborough's railway heritage. Rev Paten had visited the USA and been impressed by the number of American cities that had commemorated their debt to railways by preserving steam locomotives on plinths, and was determined to do the same for Peterborough. However, No 73050 was found to be in working order and too good to be 'stuffed', so funds were raised for its complete restoration. It was at this time that the society moved its base to the British Sugar Corporation's sidings at Peterborough and acquired its second locomotive, Hunslet 0-6-0ST *Jack's Green* from Nassington Quarries.

As time went on, signalling equipment of GNR, MR, LNER and BR origins was obtained locally during the Peterborough resignalling scheme. The signal box at Nene Junction was dismantled and eventually re-erected on the line, together with an MR box from Maxey Road, Helpston, which was moved in one piece to the society's terminus at Orton Mere. Further locomotives were added from former British Sugar stock, either by purchase or on long-term loan.

A major problem for the society by 1974 was the acute shortage of available ex-BR locomotives and, indeed, rolling stock, as most of what had been saved from the cutter's torch had been acquired by other groups. Keen to get trains running as soon as possible, having paid out a considerable sum for the line, the situation looked bleak, since apart from No 73050 and assorted small industrial shunting locos there was no immediate prospect of being able to operate a meaningful and profitable service. The solution that presented itself came in the shape of ex-Swedish Railways 'S1' Class oil-fired 2-6-4T loco No 1928, to haul continental rolling stock. Although this was higher and wider than British stock and modifications were therefore needed to platforms and bridges to allow for the continental loading gauge, a feasibility study showed it to be achievable.

The new 'Wansford Steam Centre' was opened at Easter 1974 and between then and 1977 the line was upgraded to passenger-carrying standard. The first passenger train ran on 1 June 1977, hauled by a French locomotive, *Nord*, and No 1178, another Swedish tank loco, pulling a set of ex-BR electric multiple unit coaches owned by the Southern Electric Group.

By the 1980s the Nene Valley Railway was firmly established and no longer dependant on 'foreigners' to keep its trains running, although the continental influence was still strongly in evidence. In fact, the NVR boasts 'one of the most varied collections of locomotives and rolling stock in the UK, if not in the world', a claim justified by examples from Britain, including SR 'Battle of Britain' 4-6-2 No 34081 *92 Squadron*, BR 7MT 4-6-2 No 70000 *Britannia* and BR 5MT 4-6-0 No 73050, now named *City of Peterborough*, supported by a dozen or

Top: Standing on shed is the NVR's pioneer loco, BR Class 5 4-6-0 No 73050.

Above: Un-named in her BR days, but now owned by Peterborough City Council, No 73050 was named *City of Peterborough* by the Mayor of Peterborough on 28 August 1972.

Right: BR Class 5 No 73050 brings a train into Wansford station during August 1984.

Far right: Wansford station is all quiet between trains during April 1987.

Above: Having been restored at Bridgnorth on the Severn Valley Railway in the late 1970s, 'Britannia' Class 'Pacific' No 70000, *Britannia* herself, is seen at her home on the Nene Valley Railway in August 1984.

Above right: Also in April 1987, 'J94' Class 0-6-0ST No 68081 waits in the sidings, with diesel-hydraulic 0-4-0 shunter No 8368 *Horsa* in the background.

so 'industrials', as well as locos from France, Belgium, Germany, Poland, Italy, Denmark, Sweden and Norway.

The 2,300-acre Nene Park, through which the railway runs extends from the city centre out as far as the A1, alongside the River Nene, and includes Ferry Meadows Country Park. Linking the city with Wansford station and running through the park is the well-signposted footpath of the Nene Way. These parkland areas with their lakes and quiet places are a haven for wildlife, and the nature reserve in Wansford Tunnel cutting is home to rare plants unique to this part of the country. Thus the NVR fits well as a public amenity in addition to providing transport, thereby contributing to and being part of everyone's leisure interests.

Although the NVR started with few facilities, by 1980 the station at Wansford had been developed to include a spacious new shop and nearby turntable. A locomotive shed was under construction, Stage 1 of which boasts a 60-foot, two-road building with workshop, much of which comprises the former Peterborough Pig Market building – a gift from the Council! There are plans to expand this facility to a four-road shed of double the length.

The country station at Wansford was closed to passengers on 1 July 1957, and soon afterwards the footbridge and down-side station canopy were removed. The

18-inch-high platform was shortened and the island platform demolished. Freight in the form of iron ore traffic from Nassington continued until the closure of the quarries in 1971. By then, the Wansford station buildings had been sold and the track was lifted. The closed signal box had had its rodding disconnected and the locking room was being used as a chicken coop.

The 'last train over the line' was organised by the Peterborough Railway Society in conjunction with the RCTS and ran on 4 November 1972. For most country stations that would have been the end. Wansford, however, was fortunate in being taken over by the railway society in 1974 and reborn as the headquarters of the Nene Valley Railway.

By the mid-1980s, the growth in popularity of the NVR brought the long-sought result of reinstating a passenger service over the 'Fletton branch', the BR freight line connecting the British Sugar Corporation's factory with the East Coast Main Line at Fletton Junction, south of Peterborough. A regular DMU shuttle is operated on summer weekends from Peterborough station to the NVR station at Orton Mere, a quarter of a mile beyond Longueville Junction. With the NVR now effectively reconnected with the BR network, railway society 'specials' from far and wide have brought a variety of locomotives along the Fletton branch, in addition to the sugar beet pulp trains from the sugar factory.

In July 1984 Longueville became a junction again, as the NVR commenced re-laying the line back towards Peterborough East over the old LNWR trackbed to a new station on the site of the long-gone engine sheds, thereby giving the NVR direct access to BR metals over its own extended line. The new station of Peterborough Nene Valley is the eastern terminus of the railway and in addition to its main arrivals and departures platform, Platform 1, it boasts a small bay platform, Platform 2, where lovingly restored goods wagons are kept for use on special occasions. On hand is a water tower from Barking, East London, and for the thirsty passengers a refreshment room serves drinks and snacks. There is also a shop and display area within this recently refurbished station interior, where visitors can view the history of the railway buildings that previously occupied the site.

Now describing itself as 'Britain's International Steam Railway', the NVR also boasts an impressive array of carriages including pre-nationalisation and international examples, as well as a large collection of wagons and other vehicles, including an impressive 40-ton steam crane.

Along the railway, more recent developments include a new station built at Yarwell Junction and opened in 2007, which affords passengers the opportunity to disembark and visit the nearby local villages of Yarwell and Nassington.

Outside the sheds in August 1991, 'J94' Class 0-6-0ST No 68081 awaits her next duty alongside Polish Railways 2-10-0 No 7173.

The Nene Valley's 'signature loco', City of Peterborough, heads a train over the River Nene into Wansford station at the end of another successful day's steaming in August 1984.

Special days occur on heritage lines fairly regularly, such is the nature of hard work and enthusiasm. However, very special days come along less often, but when they do…!

Just such a day came on 11 March 2010 at Sheringham, when, as the banner clearly states, reconnection to the national network was achieved just 46 years after the track was removed.

BR Standard 4-6-2 No 70013 *Oliver Cromwell*, hauling 'The Broadsman', a special operated by the Railway Touring Company from London King's Cross, is seen making the first public service crossing on that eventful day. *Cliff Thomas*

In the latter half of the 19th century the total monopoly enjoyed by the Great Eastern Railway in providing services throughout East Anglia was abruptly challenged when several small railway schemes in various parts of Norfolk where united under the influence of the Great Northern and Midland railway companies, which, jealous of the GER's ever more profitable holiday traffic to the seaside resorts of north-east Norfolk, intervened in 1893 by forming the Midland & Great Northern Railway. This new and very independent company lived on past the 'Grouping' until in 1936 the LNER assumed control and sweeping changes were soon made to working practices and locomotive livery. Under BR stewardship, the consequences of being a limited cross-country route were again felt, and closure began in 1952, although it was one winter weekend in 1959 that saw, almost in one fell swoop, virtually all of the system operated by the old M&GNR closed, as its lines became the first candidates for complete closure.

Faced with such a prospect, a group of enthusiasts were already banding together to venture into something that was completely new at the time, preservation, and of no less than a complete standard-gauge line. The Midland & Great Northern Joint Railway Society was founded in 1959 with the aim of preserving and running public services over the condemned route, and the line now known as the North Norfolk Railway was born, and with it the tasks of organising volunteers, raising funds, seeking publicity and restoring historic items of railwayana, particularly those concerned with East Anglia, began in earnest.

Initially the only trains to run were members' trains, but by May 1976 a Light Railway Order had been obtained and paying passengers could be carried along the society's 3 miles of track bordering the Norfolk coast. A seven-year restoration programme came to fruition in October 1977 when 'J15' 0-6-0 No

The crossing is witnessed, it would seem, by just about the entire community of Sheringham! No 70013 eases towards Sheringham station. *Cliff Thomas*

564 (BR number 65462) from the GER was ceremoniously recommissioned by Dr Coiley, then Keeper of the National Railway Museum.

The new line runs between the coastal town of Sheringham and the market town of Holt, a distance of 5¼ miles. Major projects to restore the railway have included the reconstruction of the station building from Stalham in its

Arrival at Holt proved just as interesting for onlookers! *Cliff Thomas*

new location at Holt, together with restoration of the station's signal box and the building of new carriage sheds near Holt to supplement the main restoration sheds at Weybourne.

Currently the railway's operational steam locos include GWR '5600' Class 0-6-2T No 5619 (on loan from the Telford Steam Railway) and '5700' Class 0-6-0PT No L99, BR 2-10-0 9F No 92203, and Hunslet 0-6-0ST No 3777. Locos undergoing overhaul or restoration include LNER Class 'B12' 4-6-0 No 61572 and GER Class 'J15' 0-6-0 No 65462. 'WD' 'Austerity' 2-10-0 No 90775 is awaiting restoration, needing an extensive boiler overhaul.

Opposite page top and left:
A pair of images that feature 'N7' Class 0-6-2T No 69621 at Holt in charge of the superbly turned out rake of of Ex-LNER 'Quad Art' cariages set no 74 plus nearest the loc, BYP 6843 a BY Pigeon Brake also of LNER origin. *Cliff Thomas*

The diesel fleet includes BR Class 07 and Class 11 locos, together with Bo-Bo Class 25 No 25057, A1A-A1A Class 31 No 31207 and Co-Co Class 47 No 47367.

The very distinctive mustard-yellow livery of the M&GNR was carried by the mainstays of the through express traffic, the somewhat underpowered 4-4-0s from a Midland design of 1894, which were often required to struggle over the severe gradients of the line with trains of 15 coaches or more. Unfortunately no locomotive of this class has survived, so the North Norfolk Railway has been denied what would have been an essential item in its collection.

Main picture: Double-heading through the Norfolk countryside on 8 March 2009. Leading is 4F 0-6-0 No 44421, one of over 700 built, followed by 'N7' Class 0-6-2T No 69621 once again. *Cliff Thomas*

Below: Same location, same day and same carriages but different motive power! In fact, this is the other end of the same train, and the loco is visiting 'N2', Class 0-6-2T (BR No 69523) masquerading as GNR No 744. *Cliff Thomas*

NORTH YORKSHIRE MOORS RAILWAY

My move from the Black Country to the beautiful city of York in 1975 opened up new and exciting possibilities as the steam railway preservation movement was already growing from strength to strength. From my new home I was ideally positioned to gain easy access to steam centres growing in popularity with each passing year.

Ex-BR Class 4MT 2-6-4T No 80135, designed at Brighton and introduced in 1951, graces the North Yorkshire Moors at Moorgates with a train for Pickering.

The North Yorkshire Moors Railway is one such. The line originally connected Whitby on the North Sea coast with Pickering, a market town on the southern edge of the North Yorkshire Moors, by way of a branch that leaves the Whitby to Middlesbrough line at Grosmont, climbing steeply to cross the National Park. Indeed, the slog up the hill to the first stop at Goathland requires the train crews to tackle the 1 in 49 gradient from a standing start. Beyond Goathland, passengers can enjoy the remote open moorland before following Newtondale down to the bustling terminus town of Pickering.

Grosmont station in August 1977, showing the adjacent BR signal box and Esk Valley line from Middlesbrough to Whitby.

The line itself is historic, dating back to 1835 as part of the Whitby & Pickering Railway. Being the culmination of attempts to halt the demise of the whaling and shipbuilding port of Whitby, which was better connected to the rest of the country by sea than by land, it was felt that improved links with the interior would regenerate the town and save the port from further decline. Following the success of the Stockton & Darlington Railway, itself benefiting from a number of Whitby backers, a decision was taken to establish the committee that would lead to the Whitby & Pickering Railway Bill receiving Royal Assent on 6 May 1833. Intending to connect its new line with York and beyond, a delegation, including the engineer George Stephenson, met with representatives of the proposed York to Leeds railway, headed by none other than the 'Railway King', George Hudson, to lobby in favour of a link to Pickering. The Whitby & Pickering was absorbed into Hudson's York & North Midland Railway empire soon after, and the town flourished as a holiday resort as a result of Hudson's investment in hotels and roads, as well as becoming the focus of new industries centred on quarrying and mining, for which the new railway provided cheap and easy transport.

Planned by George Stephenson, his three main achievements on the line were the cutting of a 120-yard tunnel at Grosmont, believed to be one of the oldest railway tunnels in the world and now used as a footpath between the station and the engine sheds and works; the construction of a rope-worked incline system at Beck Hole; and the crossing of the notoriously deep and marshy Fen Bog, using sheep fleeces on a bed of timber.

Originally horse-worked up the Beck Hole incline (now a footpath), a stationary steam engine was later used, even after the rest of the line had been converted to locomotives by George Hudson. The Beck Hole incline was closed in 1865 as steam locos could not operate over it, and a deviation completed to Goathland, together with a new station in that village.

The whole line from Malton to Whitby was closed to passenger services in 1965 as part of the Beeching cuts, following heavy financial losses, though the Malton to Pickering section remained freight-only until July 1966. The tracks from Pickering to Grosmont, however, were never lifted, as almost immediately attempts were initiated to reopen the line, and although these early initiatives came to nothing the movement did lead to the formation of the North Yorkshire Moors Railway Preservation Society in 1967, which became the North York Moors Historical Railway Trust in 1971. The initial 'railway weekends', when steam trains ran with privately owned stock, permitted only members to travel; however, as 'instant membership' for one year was available on the spot, rapid growth in membership to more than 6,000 was soon achieved. Successful fundraising supported by local people underpinned the railway's commitment to offer a much-needed public service throughout the year, especially in winter, when the roads across the high moors are blocked with snow. Thus the early success of the venture was assured, leading to the reopening of the line and steam trains echoing again across the lonely moors in 1973.

Preserved 'A4' 'Pacific' No 60007 *Sir Nigel Gresley* races past Moorgates after leaving Goathland and heading for Pickering.

Increasing public awareness of and interest in wildlife and the natural environment during the 1970s, together with greater participation in walking and outdoor pursuits in general, served to engender support for a preserved steam railway through the North York Moors National Park. Grants from Government and European Regional Development funds secured the future of the line, supporting as they did one of its major objectives – to open up areas of the National Park to walkers without jeopardising the environment by a substantial increase in motor traffic.

In July 1975 at Grosmont station, Stanier 'Black 5' No 5428, later to be named *Eric Treacy*, leaves Platform 3 to take her train out across the level crossing towards Pickering.

The mid-1970s saw rapid increases in passenger journeys and therefore in revenue, even though by 1978 only 20% of train journeys were steam-hauled. Diesel locomotives and especially DMUs were responsible for the lion's share of the mileage, suggesting that passengers were primarily attracted by an interesting train ride, with the possibility of steam as an added bonus. By 1979 the railway had become the fastest-growing tourist attraction in the North East.

Steam locomotive stock in those early days consisted of a handful of 'industrials', but by 1981 the list was far more impressive, including LMS 'Black 5' Nos 5428 *Eric Treacy* and 4767 *George Stephenson*, 'K1' 2-6-0 No 2005, SR 'S15' 4-6-0 No 841 *Greene King*, two 'West Country' Class 4-6-2s, Nos 34010 *Sidmouth* and 34027 *Taw Valley*, NER 'T3' 0-8-0 No 63460, and BR 9F 2-10-0

Grosmont station in August 1977 sees 'Black 5' No 4767, now named *George Stephenson*, waiting to enter the station, while in the background ex-NER 'T2' 0-8-0 No 2238 prepares to leave.

Ex-GNR pannier tank No 1247 gets the signal to leave Grosmont in October 1978.

During April 1977 ex-NER 'P3' 0-6-0 No 2392 takes a guards-van away from Grosmont station.

No 92134, forming a total of about 25 locomotives.

The line's 18-mile length now makes it the second-longest standard-gauge preserved line in Britain, after the Taunton to Minehead line of the West Somerset Railway (25 miles). The steep gradient and long distance involved reinforce the need for real power, so the larger locos are often employed to thrilling effect. Regular performers are the two 'Black 5s', the LNER 'K1' and, a recent addition, ex-S&D 2-8-0 No 13809.

Reaching the NYMR from York involves driving north-east up the A64 towards Malton, then turning north along the A169 to Pickering, a journey of about 25 miles. To do the line justice and experience the steep gradient, it is best to continue on the A169 towards Whitby. The drive is worthwhile in itself, over the beautiful North Yorkshire Moors, passing the sinister radar housing of the early warning station at RAF Fylingdales, which has replaced the more aesthetically pleasing 'golfballs'.

The tiny road down to Grosmont can be missed if your attention is too much on the lovely moors but, once there, the village is a worthy starting point from which to explore this gem of a railway. The station itself is welcoming, with an excellent pub right by the level crossing and a very homely tea room on the platform, both offering good value.

Catering on the Moors Line had its beginnings in the station buffet and on-train trolley service, but by 1981, following the acquisition of 1960-built Metro-Cammell 'Pullman' 1st Class parlour cars Nos E327 and E328, previously 'Opal' and 'Garnet', followed by a GWR-design inspection saloon, then the Pullman kitchen car No E318E 'Robin', the 'North Yorkshire Pullman' was in business. The Pullmans were repainted in their former 'umber and cream' livery for the 1982 season and the exclusive dining train was timetabled to operate every Wednesday between mid-May and mid-September over the full 18 miles from Pickering station and return. A full five-course dinner (with choices) and coffee, everything being cooked on board, was priced at £11.50 per person, inclusive of the rail fare, and a full bar service and extensive wine list was available. The service was an instant success, with the 84-seat Pullman train proving so popular that reservation was essential well in advance to secure a seat. With the acquisition of the Deltic Preservation Society's two 'Deltics', Nos 55009 and 55019, it is hoped that the 'North Yorkshire Pullman' will be able to recreate the style of the East Coast Main Line Pullman services of the 1960s and '70s. With visiting high-profile 'guests' forming an added attraction in the summer months, the 'railway over the moors'

draws ever greater numbers of steam tourists of all ages to the beautiful North Yorkshire Moors.

The journey up to Goathland from Grosmont is always exhilarating, culminating in the 1 in 49 heave into the station itself. Disembark here if you like – there are lovely walks back down to Grosmont either up and over the moor from beside the station or by walking through the village to the Mallyan Spout Hotel, from beside which a path leads down to the River Esk passing close to the impressive waterfall from which the hotel gets its name. This route will take you to the incline that was the original route of the railway, before entering Grosmont once more. Goathland station and the village itself attract many visitors due to being featured in Yorkshire Television's *Heartbeat* series and in the first 'Harry Potter' film.

Above: Ex-Lambton Railway 0-6-2T No 29 storms out of the station in April 1978.

Left: No 29 races past Grosmont shed with her train for Pickering in June 1975.

Below: Ex-WD 'Austerity' 2-10-0 No 3672 attacks the rising gradient out of Grosmont station in October 1990.

Alternatively stay on board the train to travel over the moors, then through deep valleys to find tiny 'halts' at Levisham, nearly 2 miles from the village that gives it its name, and Newton Dale, a remote 'request stop' – both offering the temptation of lovely walks through heather or forest. Finally there is the run down into Pickering town itself, to complete what I consider one of the great preserved-line journeys – superb scenery, a long ride giving excellent value for money and locos working hard over a route that makes serious demands on men and machines.

Above: An experiment in smoke deflection: 'Black 5' No 4767 *George Stephenson* wears wooden deflectors in the sidings at Grosmont during April 1978.

Above right: Class 'Q6' 6F No 63395 of 1913 vintage stands outside the shed.

Right: Within the shed and workshop area, Class 'B1' No 61264 has been receiving attention.

Hauling 'The Moorlander', No 2238 attracts admirers as she hauls her train into Goathland during August 1977.

Ex-S&D 2-8-0 No 53809 blasts away from Grosmont station.

Above left: At Goathland station in October 1976 ex-NER 'T2' Class No 2238 passes the signal box heading for Pickering.

Above: Later the same day No 2238 takes the single-line token ready for the run down the hill back to Grosmont.

Inset left: Passing through the beautiful North Yorkshire Moors countryside near Beck Hole during September 1991 is ex-SR 'S15' Class No 841.

Left: Also near Beck Hole is ex-BR Standard Class 4MT No 76079.

From what I always considered to be my temporary home in Walsall, Staffordshire, the journey to Bridgnorth and the Severn Valley Railway was a mere 22 miles, though my more usual route took me and my little van, which served as a weekend 'mobile home', straight from work in Wolverhampton on Friday evenings to the Shropshire steam haven, a distance of less than 15 miles. My visits began in 1972 and soon became a regular pilgrimage.

The Severn Valley Railway, incorporated into the Great Western Railway in the 1870s, had operated for more than 100 years, but had never been a successful commercial operation. Carrying only limited numbers of passenger trains, it operated largely as an agricultural freight line with coal traffic from the Highley area, but the rise of road haulage in the 1930s signalled disaster for the line's freight services and it was eventually closed in 1963.

Ex-GWR 0-6-0PT No 5784 passes beneath lower-quadrant semaphore signals with a train from Bridgnorth in October 1977.

The formation of the Severn Valley Railway dates from 1965 in the shape of the Severn Valley Railway Society of Kidderminster. Quickly raising funds, the first 5-mile section out of Bridgnorth to Alveley was purchased, and by 1967 the first rolling stock, an engine and four coaches, had been received. Three further years spent overcoming considerable difficulties, not least of which was the obtaining of the required legal authority – a Light Railway Order from the Department of the Environment – was rewarded when the line from Bridgnorth to Hampton Loade opened for passenger services in May 1970, initially using Collett 3MT 0-6-0 No 3205, a class of loco introduced in 1930. By the end of the first season 64,000 passenger journeys had been recorded. Numbers increased with each year and in 1972 passenger journeys had reached 130,000 by the end of July. The line was extended to Highley in April 1974 and on to Bewdley a month later. The stock of locomotives increased rapidly from the start and soon numbered 20, based at Bridgnorth. In 1973 these included LNER 2-6-0 No 3442 *The Great Marquess*, the preserved example of Gresley's 'K4' Class introduced in 1937 for use on the West Highland Line. Prior to their

Left: Work in progress is passed by 2-6-4T No 80079.

Above: A GWR notice near Bridgnorth warns of the penalty of 'forty shillings, and in default of payment to one month's imprisonment' for the offence of trespassing upon the railway.

At Hampton Loade station in October 1977 ex-GWR pannier tank No 5784 is prepared to take a train back to Bridgnorth.

introduction loads of more than 220 tons had required piloting, but the first of the new class, No 3441 *Loch Long*, soon demonstrated their ability to haul loads of up to 300 tons without assistance. No 3442 returned to service in 1973 after an extensive overhaul and renewal programme, its last steaming having been in 1967!

Also 'on roll' were Longmoor Military Railway 2-10-0 No 600 *Gordon*, LMS Ivatt 4MT 2-6-0 No 43106, LMS Ivatt 2MT 2-6-0 Nos 46443 and 46521, GWR locos Class '2251' 0-6-0 No 3205, Class '51xx' 2-6-2T No 5164, Class '57xx' 0-6-0PT No 5764, Class '45xx' 2-6-2T No 4566, Class '41xx'

No 5784 is seen making
the same journey five
years earlier in 1972.

2-6-2T No 4141, 4-6-0 No
7819 *Hinton Manor*, 4-6-0
No 4930 *Hagley Hall*, and BR
Class 4MT 2-6-4T No 80079,
together with a small collection
of industrial locomotives and
an already impressive array of
coaches and other rolling stock
including a steam crane and
complete breakdown train for
emergencies.

By 1981 the steam
stock had increased to 30
locomotives, including two
LMS 'Black 5s', Nos 5000
and 45110 *RAF Biggin Hill*,
8F No 8233, GWR No 6960
Raveningham Hall and GWR
No 7812 *Erlestoke Manor*,
together with further additions
to the 'industrials' and coaching
stock.

4MT No 43106 heads
along the Severn Valley
in 1974.

The Severn Valley Railway
has always prided itself in
preserving its GWR roots,
including the operation of
GWR-style lower-quadrant
signals throughout, operated
from signal boxes bearing their
original GWR nameplates
(except at Bridgnorth, which
has a replica). The line's route
along the scenic river valley
through the tiny villages of
Eardington, Hampton Loade,

Ex-GWR 2-6-2T No
4566 brings a train
towards Bridgnorth in
October 1977.

Highley and Arley to Bewdley
allowed easy access for the
photographer, who could
follow the line by means of
the tiny lanes leading from the
B4363, B4555 and the B4194
to lovingly restored country
stations along this accurately
recreated rural branch line.

Visiting Bridgnorth and
the SVR in the early 1970s
was always a joy, partly for the opportunity it gave to relive steam days in the
beautiful Shropshire countryside, but also the chance to meet up with friends
from Bolton with whom I had shared the final years of steam in the North West.
Gathering together in Bridgnorth for a weekend or a longer time during the
holidays and camping along the river near Eardington or Hampton Loade, we
would wallow in the nostalgia of the steam era.

The SVR's collection of lovingly restored locos came to include one of my
favourites, that workhorse of the LMS, Stanier 'Black 5' No 45110, with its
connection to my former home shed at Bolton in the final days of BR steam

0-6-0PT No 5764 heads for Bridgnorth.

Ex-WD saddle tank No 193 travels in the opposite direction during October 1977.

running. What a mix of relief and pride to see her still going strong! She is one of the fewer than 20 lucky survivors from a class that numbered almost 850 in the early 1960s. Perhaps even more remarkable is the fact that in the early 1970s the SVR's Stanier 8F 2-8-0 No 8233 was the only working survivor of her class in Britain, when only 10 years earlier there had been more than 650.

Bridgnorth station and engine shed always felt so welcoming. No one chased you away from the locos. 'Health and Safety', that battle cry of the killjoys, did not exist. I and others like me were free to wander, free to photograph and, if we wanted to, even free to touch!

Open access to the main stations of Bridgnorth and later Bewdley provided a wealth of photo opportunities in those early days, with a wide variety of locomotive types being put through their paces by enthusiastic crews.

After four years work, March 1977 saw the completion of the restoration and rebuilding of perhaps the most complicated 2 miles of privately owned preserved railway signalling in Britain, when the two ex-GWR signal boxes controlling movements into and out of Bewdley station were passed as 'very satisfactory' by the Railway Inspector. One of the stated aims of the SVR is to enable as many people as possible to learn about and participate in the operation of a railway, and SVR signalmen are delighted to show visitors around at quiet times and to explain the workings of their sophisticated new equipment, which enables modern safety requirements to be met while preserving an outward appearance of the age of steam.

After a busy day along the tracks, evenings spent enjoying the hospitality in the local pubs would be enhanced by the camaraderie of railway staff and volunteers comparing stories and reliving the day's highlights. With the coal fires burning and impromptu singing of railway songs creating an unforgettably nostalgic atmosphere, the time passed in a rosy glow. Songs I particularly enjoyed were 'Green All The Way', a folksy number reliving express steam days on the main line, and my favourite, 'Bring Back a Black 5 For Me', sung to the tune of 'My Bonnie Lies Over The Ocean'. Happy days in the 1970s, helping to ease the pain felt since 1968!

Of course, when visiting preserved lines such as the Severn Valley Railway, with its picturesque stations and pristine locomotives, seemingly brought back from the grave to breathe steam once more for an adoring public, it is all too easy to neglect another aspect of railway preservation that often goes on unnoticed 'behind the

Right: Having spent some time at Bolton shed during the last days of steam on BR, 'Black 5' No 45110 brings back happy memories in August 1978.

Above: The crew of No 45110 wait for their signal at Bridgnorth in August 1978.

Right and above right: On 11 October 2008, exactly 40 years to the day since the end of steam on BR, the SVR ran a 1T57 'Fifteen Guinea' anniversary special, headed by No 45110 *RAF Biggin Hill.* The train was driven by the winner of a competition organised jointly by Silver Link Publishing, Steam Railway magazine and W. H. Smith.

scenes'. That is the skilled and costly business of actually repairing and restoring the locos and rolling stock. Since the emergent society took over the site of Bridgnorth station and the associated goods yard in 1967, the SVR's Locomotive Department has evolved into a fully fledged locomotive repair depot, able to deal with almost any maintenance issue that may arise, with the exception of certain boiler work and re-tyring, for which resort is made to outside contractors. In addition to the depot's extensive 'in-house' commitments, the SVR's expertise is made available to the wider railway preservation movement, should repairs and maintenance be required to their locomotives. Such

The scene alongside Bridgnorth station in August 1978 as locos are coaled.

was the case during 1980 when Leander Locomotive Ltd decided to make use of the SVR's services to carry out an examination and overhaul of its 'Jubilee' No 5690. Following a very busy year that had included turns on BR's 'Cumbrian Coast Express' and 'Cumbrian Mountain Express', as well as appearing at the 'Rocket 150' celebrations at Rainhill, *Leander* was moved to Bridgnorth to work trains during the August Bank Holiday and Autumn Steam Gala weekends, to be followed by a complete overhaul and general repair, thus prolonging her active life well into the future.

By 1984 the SVR had extended its operation from Bewdley the 3½ miles to Kidderminster, thus connecting with BR for its services to Birmingham and Worcester and giving a total of 16½ of railway, six stations, 40 locomotives, 60 coaches and more than 60 wagons. Since that extension, giving a route of 16 miles, the plan has been to develop the railway as a major national and international tourist attraction, the success of which is reflected in the fact that it now carries in the region of 250,000 passengers each year.

To maintain such a facility, a boiler repair shop has been created at Bridgnorth and carriage restoration, repair and maintenance facilities established at Bewdley and Kidderminster, where a carriage washing plant was also added in 2003. More recently, in 2006, Kidderminster Town station was completed with the addition of a glazed concourse canopy and new refreshment and hospitality facilities.

In 2007 the new Visitor Centre at Highley was opened to the public. Named 'The Engine House', it is home to the railway's reserve collection of steam locomotives, as well as providing a venue for railway-themed exhibitions. From the appropriately named

Below: A track gang at work in the coaling yard at Bridgnorth.

Bottom: 4MT No 43106 takes a rest during 1974.

A multiple coupled loco movement in the yard, with WD saddle tank No 193 bringing them in during 1974.

Right: 2MT No 46521 leaves Bridgnorth station in 1974.

Far Right: 3F No 47383 leaves the coaling yard ready for her next assignment, also during 1974.

Ex-GWR 2-6-2 tank No 4566 backs onto her train.

No 4566 runs round her carriages ready for her next trip during August 1978.

3F No 47383 powers away from Bridgnorth in 1974.

4MT No 43106 runs round her train at Bewdley in 1974.

Right: Ex-LNER 'K4'
2-6-0 No 3442 *The
Great Marquess* waits at
the platform.

Far right: 'Black 5'
No 45110 enters
Bridgnorth station in
August 1978.

'WD' ex-LMR 2-10-0
No 600 *Gordon* brings
a train into Bewdley,
then departs again for
Bridgnorth in 1974.

'Buffers' restaurant, a balcony affords the visitor wonderful panoramic views of the Severn Valley, or the opportunity to simply sit and watch the trains go by.

The kernel of the SVR's success as a driving force of British railway preservation is the attraction of the 'perfect image' of a branch-line railway.

The original South Devon Railway reached Plymouth by way of Totnes from Newton Abbott in 1849. It was a 'broad-gauge' (7ft 0¼in) railway engineered by Isambard Kingdom Brunel and designed to be worked by the 'atmospheric' system, an experiment whose failure caused financial problems for the company for many years. Its branches included the Dartmouth & Torbay Railway, which reached Kingswear in 1864, and the Buckfastleigh, Totnes & South Devon Railway, completed by 1872. The company was amalgamated with the GWR on 1 February 1876.

Left: A glimpse of what might have been and possibly may yet be again! No 4555 is seen at Ashburton terminus on 22 August 1967 before this section of line was severed by the A38 trunk road.

Today's South Devon Railway is the 7-mile standard-gauge branch of the former GWR line running along the valley of the River Dart between Buckfastleigh and Totnes. Formerly known as the Dart Valley Railway, the preservation body known as the Dart Valley Light Railway Ltd had drawn up plans to reopen the line even before its eventual closure in 1958 for passenger trains and 1962 for freight services. Nevertheless, it was seven years before the line was fully operational again due to the

It is hard to believe that, when these three shots were taken of '1400' Class 0-4-2T No 1420 in the yard at Buckfastleigh and No 4555 at a quiet Buckfastleigh on 22 August 1967, steam was still running in day-to-day service on BR main-line metals! *All John Stretton*

problems that had mounted up during those years of neglect. These included the inevitable vandalism, the absence of a signalling system and no access to Totnes station.

The first train ran in 1967 and the line's excellent prospects were immediately apparent, with 14,000

Another early days but undated image shows Buckfastleigh south signal box and signalling under construction. *Peter Townsend collection*

visitors recorded in that year, followed by 35,000 in 1968. The first full public service began at Easter 1969 followed by a ceremonial reopening by none other than Lord Beeching on 21 May. Attention to detail and careful selection of locos for their suitability to work on the line has produced an authentic recreation of a GWR branch line.

The locomotive stock by 1972 included several 0-6-0PTs, mainly of Collett design and dating from the 1930s, a pair of Collett 0-4-2Ts, and a pair of 2-6-2Ts of Churchward design dating back to 1924. A recent arrival on the line was 4-6-0 No 7827 *Lydham Manor*, rescued from Barry after a stay of four years.

By 1974 the Dart Valley Light Railway Company Ltd was operating not one but two preserved lines, the second being the Torbay Steam Railway, which runs between Paignton and Kingswear and had until recently been traversed by main-line trains, having been taken over from BR in December 1972. The line was built by the Dartmouth & Torbay Railway and opened as far as Churston in 1861 and to Kingswear in 1864. It was always operated by the South Devon Railway and was amalgamated with it in 1872.

A general view of Buckfastleigh from the footbridge a few years later shows considerable progress. *Peter Townsend collection*

Beginning operations on 1 January 1973, the Torbay Steam Railway was an instant success, with 360,000 passenger journeys being completed in that first year. Both lines benefit from running through beautiful scenery, which includes superb coastal stretches and the lush valley of the River Dart, with the Dartmoor Hills on the horizon. The half-hour, 7-mile runs are considered 'just right' for maintaining passenger interest.

Staverton Station in August 1970 shows considerable evidence of TLC! *John Stretton*

By 1979 work was well advanced on the building of a permanent station for the Dart Valley trains at Totnes Riverside, and the development of a steam centre at Buckfastleigh, with extra siding space and a new workshop that would make considerable improvements to the efficiency of loco overhaul and maintenance. By 1982 the combined operations of the two Dart Valley lines put them in the top five busiest preserved railways in the UK, with the Torbay & Dartmouth (as the steam railway was then known) having weathered the economic recession and recorded increased passenger numbers once more, benefiting from the upturn in tourism in the Paignton area of Devon and its close working relationship with BR. In more recent times the railway changed its name to the Paignton & Dartmouth Steam Railway, then the Dartmouth Steam Railway & Riverboat Company, though it remains the property of the Dart Valley Railway Company plc. It boasts a special attraction in the form of a combined steam train ride from Paignton to Kingswear connecting with a ferry journey across the River Dart from Kingswear to the beautiful old town of Dartmouth, whose station is unique

Below left and right: Looking across the River Dart in the summer of 1983 'Manor' Class 4-6-0 No 7827 Lydham Manor can be seen in the process of running round.

Lydham Manor is seen once again later in the day approaching the terminus at Kingswear. Michael H. C. Baker

in that it has never seen a train, as passengers have always arrived by means of the ferry from Kingswear.

The ex-GWR steam locomotive stock on the Dartmouth Steam Railway includes Class '4200' 2-8-0T No 4277 *Hercules*, Class '4500' 2-6-2T No 4555 *Warrior*, Class '4575' 2-6-2T No 4588 *Trojan*, and Class '5205' 2-8-0T No 5239 *Goliath*. More recently acquired is ex-BR Class 4 4-6-0 No 75014, designed at Brighton and introduced in 1951, currently undergoing an overhaul that should eventually allow it to replace No 7827 *Lydham Manor* when the latter's boiler certificate expires.

Former GWR locomotives in operation on the South Devon Railway include Class '2251' 0-6-0 No 3205, Class '4575' 2-6-2T No 5526, Class '5700' 0-6-0PT No 5786, and Class '2884' 2-8-0 No 3803.

In addition, the railway can draw on the services of a collection of diesel shunters, main-line diesels and industrial locomotives.

Under the train shed at Kingswear is '4500' Class 2-6-2T No 4588. Peter Townsend collection.

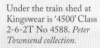

Carnforth motive power depot, coded 10A from September 1963 to the end of steam in August 1968, had long been an important base for steam locomotives; indeed, it was here that the very last job on a steam loco on BR occurred, as the fire of 'Black 5' No 44871 was dropped. Having been one of the locos used to haul 'the last steam train' on 11 August, No 44871 returned to Carnforth shed and so ended the steam era in Britain.

By 1969, however, Steamtown Railway Museum had been born, utilising the buildings of the LMS sheds. Originally acquired by Lakeside Railway Estates Co Ltd as part of a scheme to create both a live steam museum and a steam-hauled railway along the Lakeside branch, Steamtown was soon split off and became the Steamtown Railway Museum in its own right. It quickly became popular with enthusiasts as a centre for the preservation and restoration of locomotives dear to their hearts, and built up a fine collection including *Flying Scotsman*, *Mallard* and *Sir Nigel Gresley*, as well as establishing a reputation as an engineering facility capable of maintaining locos to main-line running standards. Its popularity was due in no small part to its accessibility. Easily reached by rail, being next to Carnforth railway station on the West Coast Main Line, or by road, with free car parking, it attracted visitors from far and wide, who found within the site a freedom to stroll around the engine shed among the locomotives stabled there, climb onto the footplates or enjoy a ride behind the preserved locos on the depot's own stretch of line. Footplate rides were a particular favourite.

The imposing concrete coaling plant that dominates the area was built during the Second World War, apparently by Italian prisoners of war.

As the 1970s progressed and steam-hauled trains were gradually allowed

In March 1975 we see 'Black 5' No 44871, which famously hauled the 'last' BR steam train, alongside even better known stable-mate No 4472 Flying Scotsman.

Ex-LNWR 'Precedent' Class 2-4-0 No 790 *Hardwicke* is the only survivor of a class of 166 locos built at Crewe during the period 1874-82.

back onto the railway, so Steamtown flourished, and its importance in servicing the growing number of locos being used on steam specials in the North of England increased. No longer isolated, as a result of the opening up to steam of the routes to York via Bentham, Settle Junction and Leeds, and to Barrow by means of the former Furness Railway line through Ulverston, Carnforth became a major link in the preservation movement chain as it moved from a working steam museum to a vital stabling point.

May 1982 saw the coming to fruition of a remarkable project that combined past and present in a way

unprecedented in railway preservation annals. The launch of the 'Venice Simplon Orient Express' represented the culmination of years of meticulous restoration of the rolling stock to the highest of standards. This specialised engineering achievement involved the adaptation of steam-age carriages, often with 50 years or more of service behind them, to meet the vigorous mechanical specifications of heating, braking and other safety features required for day-in,

Seen from the footplate of *Flying Scotsman*, the impressive structure of the concrete coaling tower dominates the area.

day-out high-speed running, while retaining all the elegance of a bygone age of luxury rail travel. The 13 British cars in the fleet of 25 vehicles required for the two trains were entrusted to the Steamtown workshops at Carnforth, where a large carriage repair facility had been created with the capability of overhauling rolling stock to the highest standards.

Since then, Steamtown's expertise has been in demand to restore and overhaul a variety of passenger rolling stock, including the out-shopping of the National Railway Museum's 1913-built 1st Class Pullman parlour car 'Topaz', which went on display at the NRM from July 1984. Carnforth Steamtown has evolved from a working steam centre best known for its locomotive repair and maintenance into a highly respected commercial workshop able to undertake a variety of restoration and mechanical overhaul contracts to the highest and most exacting standards. Its facilities and the expertise of its highly skilled craftsmen and engineers have gained it a new reputation second to none in the arena of railway preservation.

An April 1977 close-up of the bearings and rods shows No 4472's BR number 60103 clearly stamped.

Its popularity with the public, however, was to be its downfall as a visitor attraction. By the 1990s its services were in great demand and commercial work was being undertaken on a scale incompatible with the 'free to roam' policy of the early years, so in 1997 the site was closed to the general public for safety reasons, though the essential work of maintaining and repairing Britain's steam fleet goes on, with locos still being fed from that massive coaling plant.

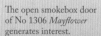

The open smokebox door of No 1306 *Mayflower* generates interest.

Above left: Steamtown's European contingent on display during April 1977: SNCF Class '231K' 'Pacific' No 231K22 *La France* occupies the turntable.

Above: Within the sheds 'Black 5' No 44932 is undergoing restoration during April 1977.

Germany is represented by 'Pacific' No 012 104-6 from the Deutsche Bundesbahn, alongside our very own much-travelled *Flying Scotsman.*

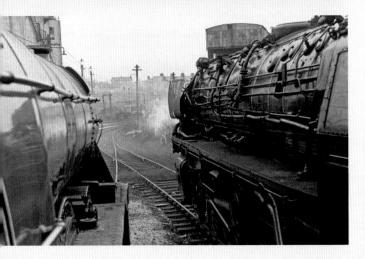

The 'free to roam' policy of those early days allowed opportunities to photograph from the footplate, as here from *Flying Scotsman,* next to the DB 'Pacific'.

In April 1977 the line-up outside the shed includes No 4472 *Flying Scotsman*, 'Black 5' No 44871 and GWR 'Modified Hall' No 6960 *Raveningham Hall*.

Rides behind a steam loco are always popular, and 'Black 5' No 45407 obliges during April 1977, on the site's running line, which features the preserved signal box from Selside on the Settle & Carlisle line.

On the other side of the site, ex-LNER 'A4' No 4498 *Sir Nigel Gresley* is seen near the coaling plant in October 1977.

Below left: Completing a famous line-up, Gresley's 'A3' No 4472 *Flying Scotsman* stands proudly on display during October 1977.

Below: Stanier 'Black 5' No 44932 is looking well and fit for work in October 1977.

STRATHSPEY RAILWAY

The weather in this part of the world has a habit of seemingly doing its best to make life difficult for visitors, especially those armed with a camera. As a 'local' in Inverness so aptly put it, 'If you can't see across the loch it's because it's raining. If you can see across the loch, it's just about to rain…' So it was at 'The Boat' on 19 August 1980, not an ideal spot to wait for trains on a rainy day, but we were rewarded with an impressive arrival in the shape of Hunslet 0-6-0ST No 60, built in 1948, with a train from Aviemore en route to Broomhill. One of a number of 'Austerity' six-coupled saddle tank engines formerly serving the National Coal Board in North East England, No 60 (Hunslet 3686/48) last worked at Dawdon Colliery in County Durham before being restored to grace the Speyside route.

Travelling more widely now, 1980 afforded an opportunity for me to visit the Highlands of Scotland and to tour the area from a base on the shores of Loch Ness near Inverness. The Strathspey Railway was a 'must visit' destination during our stay.

Originally opened in 1863 as part of the Inverness & Perth Junction Railway, later to be amalgamated into the Highland Railway, the Aviemore to Boat of Garten line was a popular excursion route in the summer from Aberdeen, but only lightly used for passenger traffic at other

times. Though the Highland lines were strategically important in support of the war effort during both the First and Second World Wars, rail traffic generally declined through the 1950s and '60s as road transport became more popular and convenient. Passenger services were finally withdrawn in 1965. Freight traffic continued for another three years, but inevitably the line was closed altogether in November 1968 as part of the Beeching cuts. So although Speyside is at the heart of the Scottish malt whisky region, along reputedly Scotland's fastest-flowing river, and though the railway was intimately linked to the export of the valued product, this 'essential of life' could not keep the railway alive.

Like so many involved in the railway preservation business, those determined to breathe life back into this magnificent stretch of line would not take 'no' for an answer. A scheme for preserving the line was first suggested in 1967. The Strathspey Railway Company was established in 1971 and the following year saw the formation of the Strathspey Railway Association, a voluntary supporting organisation, which would prove invaluable in the process of renovation and restoration in the years ahead. The line from Aviemore to Grantown was purchased from British Rail in 1972, and although the station at Boat of Garten was still standing, the track onwards to Grantown had been lifted and the bridge over the River Dulnain removed. Perseverance finally won through, when in 1978 the Strathspey Railway opened for business once more, running trains from Aviemore 'Speyside' station to Boat of Garten, thus becoming Scotland's first group-preserved line and bringing a regular steam service back to the Highland Railway after an absence of 16 years.

The first services were hauled by ex-LMS Ivatt 'Mogul' No 46464, built at Crewe in 1950, and Stanier 'Black 5' No 5025, built by the Vulcan Foundry in 1934, which had been running on the Keighley & Worth Valley Railway following its restoration by the Hunslet Engine Company in Leeds. There were also a dozen or so industrials, including a brace of Barclay 0-6-0STs and Barclay 0-6-0T No 2017, built in 1935. By 1981 'sister' LMS 'Mogul' No 46512 and Caledonian Railway 3F 0-6-0 No 828, dating from 1899 and belonging to the

The Strathspey Railway is proud of its roots, and the station with its tiny museum recalls the origin and history of this preserved line, with photographs and artefacts from years gone by.

Scottish Locomotive Preservation Trust, had been added to the collection.

Reinstating the route involved overcoming some quite major physical problems, not least of which was building a new station at Aviemore. Then there was track to re-lay at both termini, signalling to restore and telephone connections to be made.

The Strathspey Railway won a Civic Trust Award in 1976 for the restoration of Boat of Garten station, where a Highland Railway footbridge from Dalnaspidal near Pitlochry has been erected between the two platforms, replacing an identical bridge removed in the 1960s. The main building now includes a small museum mainly devoted to the Highland Railway and located in the former barrow room, which still retains its original HR varnished pine finish.

Today the Strathspey Railway operates over a 10-mile route from Aviemore to Broomhill by way of Boat of Garten, where engine sheds, coaling, watering and carriage maintenance facilities are located. The line runs through an area of outstanding natural beauty, which includes the impressive Cairngorm Mountains, home to one of Britain's rarest birds, the osprey, which famously nest close to the Boat of Garten headquarters. It has been a long-term objective of the Strathspey Railway to extend to Grantown-on-Spey, some 9 miles away, where the Highland Regional Council has plans to develop the Grantown-on-Spey (West) station site.

The line south from 'the Boat' runs along the beautiful Spey Valley, through countryside

Strathspey Railway pioneer 'Mogul' 2MT No 46464, an Ivatt design for the LMS, was built in 1950 and is owned by Dundee City Museum.

little changed since the railway was built in 1863, with its spectacular views of the Cairngorm Mountains. Snow pockets resisting the thaw often into August remind travellers that four of the five highest mountains in Britain are located within 10 miles of the railway.

At Aviemore, major developments have seen the construction of 'Speyside' station, about 500 yards north of the BR station and close to the locomotive shed. Speyside station consists of an island platform linked by a footbridge to the buildings from Dalnaspidal. A signal box on the island platform houses a frame from Wick box, while in the yard a turntable pit has been cleared of rubble to house a turntable from Kyle of Lochalsh, and nearby a HR water column from Forsinard has been erected.

'Loco of the day' No 60 returns from Broomhill with her train for Aviemore.

No 60 receives a little attention before taking the train back to Aviemore.

SWANAGE RAILWAY

Right: Rescued from Barry in 1979 and taken to Swanage in August of that year for restoration, '5600' Class 0-6-2T No 6695 returned to passenger service on Saturday 11 February 2006. No 6695 is seen here at Swanage in 2009.

Middle: The only surviving Gresley 0-6-2T 'N2' Class to survive gains admiring glances from the bank overlooking Swanage station during a visit to the railway in 2011. Smartly turned out in the livery of the Great Northern Railway, No 1744 is seen awaiting departure. *Both Michael H. C. Baker*

Below: Swanage station in the early years of the preservation period on 28 July 1982. *John Stretton*

The Swanage Railway Company, in Purbeck, Dorset, opened its line in 1885. It was operated by the London & South Western Railway, later to become part of the Southern Railway and the Southern Region of British Railways. Although the line was identified as a candidate for closure by the Branchline Committee in the 1950s, substantial opposition resulted in the proposal being shelved. The line also escaped the 1963 report by Dr Beeching, *The Reshaping of British Railways*, possibly because alternative transport in the region was so poorly developed. Never having been included in the third-rail electrification schemes prevalent in the area meant that the line was operated by Class 205 DMUs until its eventual closure in January 1972. However, only four months

later the Swanage Railway Society was formed with the aim of restoring an all-year-round community railway linked to the main line at Wareham.

After problems with BR over the lifting of the tracks in the Corfe Castle area, it having been envisaged that the land was required by Dorset County Council for a bypass round the village, demolition was halted following a 'sit-in' by local residents, although by this time only half a mile of track and 6 miles of ballast could be saved. Negotiations then continued with Dorset County Council over the intended route of its bypass and also with BR regarding purchase of the land. Meanwhile an estimate for the cost of putting the line back into operational order was given in 1974 as £105,000, a major sum of money, but the society felt that it would be in a stronger position to influence the Council's choice of route if it could purchase the trackbed. It therefore set about raising the money by a combination of commercial sponsorship, members' donations and other fund-raising activities; one appeared in *The Railway Magazine* of March 1974 in the form of the Swanage Railway Project 'Yard of Track' appeal. This invited readers to register for a number of shares in the 'Yard of Track Fund' at £2 per share, as part of the society's National Appeal to raise £20,000 towards the cost of the campaign to reopen the Swanage branch line.

Even when the national recession forced the County Council to put the Corfe Castle bypass on hold for the indefinite future, it took a decision by the 1975 Annual Swanage Town Meeting to demand a referendum on the future of Swanage station, which Swanage Council planned to knock down and turn into an 'open space with car parking facilities', before any further progress was made. The Town Council was bound by law to hold the referendum, and in July 1975 the result proclaimed that 83% of voters wished the station buildings and part of the site to be made available to the railway society. After a further six months of hard bargaining the society eventually moved into the station in February 1976 on a one-year no-prejudice lease, with the promise that a more substantial agreement would be forthcoming when the project raised the necessary capital.

Within a year the site had undergone extensive restoration, with locomotives already 'in residence' and a shop and exhibition room doing a brisk trade. The

Visiting the Swanage railway in 2006 is Beattie 2-4-0WT No 30587, seen leaving on a service to Norden in the summer of 2006. *Michael H. C. Baker*

Swanage Railway Project was no longer simply an idea. It had already begun.

A short length of line was at last opened in 1979, this being gradually extended until in 1995 the railway was reopened between Swanage and Corfe Castle. In January 2002, 30 years to the day after it was closed, the Purbeck branch was finally reopened, and later that year a Virgin Trains Class 220 'Voyager' DMU became the first main-line train to use the new track with its, albeit temporary at the time, main-line connection. Permanent connection was completed in 2007, and the first public passenger service between Wareham and Swanage since 1972 ran from London Victoria on 1 April 2009. The Swanage Railway's aim, to re-establish a daily service connected to the main line and operating along a whole branch in its original form, thus came one step closer to fruition.

Top left: 'T9' Class 4-4-0 No 30120 makes an energetic start from Swanage on 25 April 1992, with the 1430 to Harmons Cross. *John Stretton*

Top right: 'M7' 0-4-4T No 30053 Approaches Corfe Castle station on 2 September 2003.

Above: On 17 July 2010 BR Standard 2-6-4T No 80104 is seen leaving Corfe Castle.

Right: No 34028 *Eddystone* is in fine fettle as she passes beneath Corfe Castle on 17 July 2010. *All Michael H. C. Baker*

Operational steam stock includes LSWR 0-4-4T 'M7' Class No 30053, SR 4-6-2 'West Country' Class No 34028 *Eddystone*, GWR 0-6-2T '5600' Class No 6695, and BR 2-6-4T Class 4MT No 80104. Diesel stock includes three BR Bo-Bo Class 33s, Nos 33012,

33103 and 33111, together with BR 0-6-0 shunter No 08436 and two DMUs. Several other locomotives are currently undergoing restoration and overhaul, notably SR 'Battle of Britain' Class 4-6-2 Nos 34053 *Sir Keith Park*, 34070 *Manston* and 34072 *257 Squadron*, together with BR 2-6-2T Class 4MT No 80078.

Today the railway boasts 'a more intensive heritage steam and diesel timetable train service than virtually any other preserved railway', with trains running every weekend throughout the year and a full weekday service in operation between April and October, whereby visitors can travel through more than 6 miles of beautiful scenery, passing by the magnificent ruins of Corfe Castle.

Above left: Running smokebox-first this time, BR Standard 2-6-4T No 80104 is seen leaving Corfe Castle behind her on 17 July 2010. *Michael H C Baker*

Above: After arriving at Harmons Cross, then the temporary terminus, 'T9' Class 4-4-0 No 30120 runs round its train before returning to Swanage on 25 April 1992. *John Stretton*

Left: The 'Devon Belle' observation car No 14 is much travelled, having visited the USA with *Flying Scotsman* in 1969. It was not until February 2007 that the car returned to Southampton docks. Following restorative work at Ramparts works in Derby, a return to service, on the Swanage Railway, took place on Wednesday 16 July 2008. *Michael H C Baker*

SWINDON & CRICKLADE RAILWAY

Operating over a short length of the old Midland & South Western Junction Railway from Andover to Cheltenham, itself a minor railway with just under 60 route miles, the Swindon & Cricklade Railway was opened as a volunteer heritage line in 1978 and has two stations at Hayes Knoll and Blunsdon. Advertised as 'Wiltshire's only standard gauge heritage railway', it offers a round trip of approximately 4 miles at weekends and on Bank Holidays, with special events being included at times such as Easter and Christmas.

By 1981 the society was operating a rudimentary service by means of diesel-mechanical shunters and a Peckett 0-6-0ST dating from 1916, with rolling stock

Right: In glorious summer sunshine, '4300' Class 2-6-0 No 5322, in pseudo-ROD WWI livery, arrives at Blunsdon on the 1349 ex-South Meadow Lane, on 19 June 2010.

Below: 'City' Class 4-4-0 No 3440 *City of Truro* stands in Blunsdon's platform on 6 March 2005, before starting out on the next shuttle to Hayes Knoll. *Both John Stretton*

Slough Estates No. 3 accelerates hard to look the part at the head of one of the Swindon & Cricklade Railway's 'Santa Specials' on 11 December 2004. Ex-BR 03 Class No 2022 was at the other end.

consisting of an ex-GWR coach, a Brecon & Merthyr van body and four goods wagons.

Blunsdon station platform has been extended to accommodate four-coach trains and features a waiting room rescued from Malmesbury and an LMS signal box from Claydon Junction, on the Bletchley to Oxford line. A new engine shed has been erected at Hayes Knoll to accommodate locos and allow maintenance and restoration to take place under cover. The station itself is also newly constructed. Work is under way to extend the railway northwards to Cricklade

Swindon & Cricklade Railway's 'GWR175 Steam Gala' saw both north and south extensions from the previous running line. On Saturday 12 June 2010 No 5542 and auto-coach No 178 accelerate from Blunsdon with a shuttle on the southern extension. *Both John Stretton*

Above: On a warm sunny Saturday 12 June 2010, 'City' Class 4-4-0 No 3717 *City of Truro* (note the loco is now carrying its original GWR number and livery) restarts the 1419 South Meadow Lane-Blunsdon service from the Hayes Knoll stop, during the S&CR's 'GWR175 Steam Gala'.

Right: On Saturday 19 June 2010, during the second of the two 'GWR175 Steam Gala' weekends, Auto-coach No 178 stands behind No 5542 at the temporary halt at Blunsdon, ready to run another shuttle over the line south towards Swindon. *Both John Stretton*

and southwards to Mouldon Hill Country Park, Swindon.

The stock list has grown considerably from those early years, and now features GWR 3F 0-6-0PT No 3650 of Class '5700', built in 1939 and on hire from Didcot, as well as industrial locos including a pair of 0-6-0STs of Andrew Barclay design, Nos 2138 and 2139, dating from 1941/42, an 0-6-0ST by Hunslet, No 2413 of 1941 vintage, 0-6-0T No 1464 of 1921 by Hudswell Clarke, and an 0-4-0ST by Andrew Barclay, No 2354 dating from 1954.

Also available are a clutch of Class 03, 08 and 09 diesel shunters from ex-BR stock, and electro-diesel Class 73/0 No E6003, together with two multiple units and three 0-4-0 industrial diesel locomotives.

BR Mk 1 coaching stock handles all the passenger requirements, including buffet facilities, and the railway has a specially restored and adapted 'wine & dine' set for special occasions. The collection of restored goods vehicles has also grown to the point where it is now possible to run demonstration freight trains.

As seen on page 146, making its first appearance on the Swindon & Cricklade Railway, No 5322 is reminiscent of World War troop trains that once used this line, operating as the 1504 South Meadow Lane-Blunsdon on Saturday 12 June 2010, during the railway's 'GWR175 Steam Gala'.

Watched by an appreciative crowd of onlookers, 0-6-0PT No 4612 heads the 1440 Blunsdon-South Meadow Lane service through Hayes Knoll on Saturday 12 June 2010, during the railway's 'GWR175 Steam Gala'. *Both John Stretton*

WEST SOMERSET RAILWAY

The first West Somerset Railway was opened in 1862, initially between Taunton and Watchet Harbour. Although Brunel had been engaged as engineer in 1857, most of the work was done by his assistant, R. P. Brereton. On completion, the 14½ miles of broad-gauge track was leased in perpetuity to the Bristol & Exeter Railway. It ran for only eight years in broad-gauge form before being converted to standard gauge. The journey took 50 minutes over steep gradients; these often troubled the locomotives, which in the early days were stocky Bristol & Exeter Railway saddle tanks of Sir Daniel Gooch design, later succeeded by the brass and copper embellished products from Armstrong and Dean. The four trains a day in each direction stopped at the intermediate stations of Bishops Lydeard, Crowcombe (known as Heathfield until 1889), Stogumber and Witton. A further station at Norton Fitzwarren, 2 miles from Taunton, was opened in 1873.

'4200' Class 2-8-0T No 4277 rounds the curve near Watchet on the return run of a special charter on 13 July 1996. *John Stretton*

An unsuccessful plan that never came to fruition was to link the line with that of the West Somerset Mineral Railway, a standard-gauge track built to cater for the thriving mining industry exploiting the rich iron ore deposits of the Brendon Hills and exporting the ore to South Wales through the port of Watchet. The two railways thus operated independently until the WSMR was finally wound up in 1910, its rolling stock being transferred to the Great Western Railway and its track being eventually lifted in 1917 and commandeered for munitions in aid of the war effort.

Traffic on the WSR line grew steadily and an extension along the coast to Minehead was ready for traffic in 1874. The town was visited by a delegation from the GWR in 1876 after the Bristol & Exeter had been amalgamated into it, and the Chairman, Sir Daniel Gooch himself, was reportedly impressed by the railway, the town and the surrounding country. The original WSR retained its independence until 1921, when under the Railways Act it was finally amalgamated into the Great Western Railway, which in turn became the Western Region of British Railways on 1 January 1948.

Passing loops and automatic token exchange apparatus for

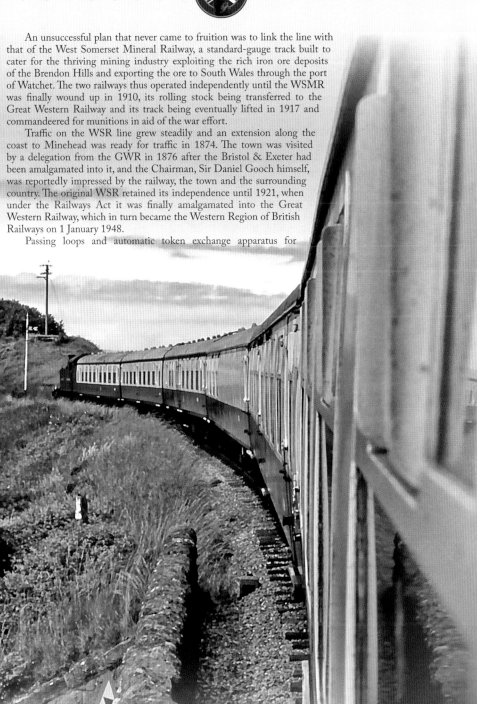

the single-line sections had been installed in the early 1930s as part of a modernisation programme, but inevitably the line was recommended for closure in Dr Beeching's 1963 report, *The Reshaping of British Railways*, and goods traffic was withdrawn by July 1964. The line was finally closed on 2 January 1971, after a life of 96½ years, despite much protest and following a week in which every item that could be used elsewhere or that might be attractive to 'collectors' had been methodically removed.

There were two 'final trains'. The 'last daylight train' was organised by the Taunton Division of the Great Western Society and carried that society's headboard and badge. Minehead Round Table ran a special 'last train', which started from Minehead at 7.30pm and returned 3 hours later. This was accompanied by the Minehead Town Band, which played at all the stations, and on its return journey left Taunton to the accompaniment of exploding detonators and was acknowledged at Watchet by the prolonged sirens of two ships in the harbour. The following day, a Sunday, saw the 'recovery train', hauled by 'Hymek' diesel-hydraulic No D7047, wend its way up the line to pick up anything that had been left behind. Successfully 'salvaged' were three ex-GWR 'Toplight' camping coaches, which had stood for several years in a siding at Blue Anchor and were intended for restoration.

Notwithstanding, in February of that same year the Minehead Railway Preservation Society organised a meeting to investigate how the line could be

Two views taken from the end of Minehead station on 16 January 1993 show a Cravens Class 105 DMU set made up of Nos 51485 and 56121. The set left the WSR in 1997 and at the time of writing is undergoing restoration at Buckley Wells Carriage shed on the East Lancashire Railway. *Gary Thornton*

reopened as a privately run railway, and by May 1971 a new West Somerset Railway Company had been formed to implement proposals for reopening the line between Taunton and Minehead.

In 1973 Somerset County Council agreed to purchase the land and permanent way from BR and to lease the operational section, including the station buildings, to the company. However, by August of that year little progress appeared to have been made towards reopening, other than the posting of explanatory notices along the line, but considerable damage had been done by vandals to fittings left by BR, and station buildings, signal boxes and permanent way huts had been broken into. Similarly there had been damage to mileposts and gradient posts along the branch and some signals had gone. That said, the trackbed was reported to be in good order and only isolated patches of weeds and other growth impeded the return of traffic. More of an obstacle were the objections raised against the proposed reopening of this interesting and beautiful line. Notable among the private individuals who voiced their concerns was a retired army officer who lived beside the line at Bishops Lydeard and who claimed that the trains would disturb badgers and rare butterflies that had settled along the line.

By 1974 a public enquiry had been convened, and met on 22 January in the Shire Hall in Taunton, where about 150 people gathered to hear objections to British Railways' application for a Light Railway Order relating to the Taunton-

The detailed information in the following captions are provided couertesy of

SIX BELLS JUNCTION

www.sixbellsjunction.co.uk

On 16 January a special train was run by Hertfordshire Rail Tours, 'The Quantock Explorer' (125 Special No. 94). Starting from Bedford at 0735, HST Set 43083 + 43054 had a good run, arriving at Bishops Lydeard right time at 1250. Passengers transferred to the waiting WSR train for the trip to Minehead behind '2251' Class 0-6-0 No 3205 and '4500' Class No 4561, arriving 13 minutes early at 1407.

The return working left Minehead at 1550, Bishops Lydeard (HST) at 1515 and arrived back in Bedford at 2154

0-6-0 No 3205 is seen at the seafront end of Minehead station about to run round the special seen in the previous photograph in preparation for a return to Bishops Lydeard and thence by the HST to Bedford. *Both Gary Thornton*

Minehead railway. The order would allow Somerset County Council, owner of the line, to apply for its powers to be transferred to the West Somerset Railway Company, to whom the line would be leased for the operation of an all-year-round commuter service between Taunton and Minehead and summer-only steam trains between Minehead and Williton. The enquiry was adjourned to 2 April after an objection from the Western National Omnibus Company was received so late that more time was needed to meet it. There were three other objections from private individuals. The bus company's objection centred around the proposed subsidy for the commuter service, which it argued would be unfair competition and might lead to the bus company in turn requesting a subsidy or having to withdraw its services.

In spite of the objections, it soon became clear that the majority of those present wholeheartedly supported the railway, as speakers in favour were frequently greeted with applause while those in opposition, including the army officer, were treated with disdain. On 2 April the enquiry duly resumed, whereupon the principal objector, the Western National Omnibus Company, withdrew its objection, citing a meeting held between it and the West Somerset Railway at which assurances had been received regarding fare structures. Following extensive evidence from both sides, the enquiry was closed for the matter to be considered further, but opinion at the time was strongly that there was a genuine demand from the public of the district for the line and that the case presented for reopening was entirely convincing.

Subsequently a Transfer Order enabling BR to transfer the railway to the County Council was granted with effect from 9 September 1975, so that the

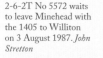

2-6-2T No 5572 waits to leave Minehead with the 1405 to Williton on 3 August 1987. *John Stretton*

'2251' Class 0-6-0 No 3205 and '4500' Class No 4561 'take refreshment' in preparation for the return trip to Bishops Lydeard with the 'Quantock Explorer' special on 16 January 1993. *Gary Thornton*

Destination accomplished for auto-coach No 178 at 7 minutes past 5! Sadly the date was not recorded. *Peter Townsend*

No 4277 approaches
Watchet station on 28
July 1999, with the 1400
Minehead-Bishops
Lydeard working. *John
Stretton*

Council could lease the operational sections to the West Somerset Railway,
effective from 31 October for 20 years. A share issue to the public of up to
650,000 ordinary shares at 10p per share was launched in 1976, with the
expectation that it would generate a significant proportion of the £82,000 that
the Directors calculated would be needed to reopen the railway and carry on
operations.

At 10.27am on Sunday 28 March 1976, five years and three months after
British Railways had closed the Taunton to Minehead branch, Lord Montagu

of Beaulieu, wearing his grandfather's top hat, flagged away the first load of fare-paying passengers from Minehead to Blue Anchor, hauled by Bagnall 0-6-0ST No 2996 *Victor*, which had been decorated with bunting and the Union Flag for the occasion. The train pulled out of Minehead station to the sound of whistles, hooters, detonators and a silver band. Pannier tank No 6412, recently purchased from the Torbay Steam Railway, was in steam at Minehead to share the subsequent trains, and on static display in one of the platforms was the Somerset & Dorset 2-8-0, which it was hoped to steam in the near future, together with the 'Hymek' diesel-hydraulic locomotive owned by the Diesel & Electric Group and the two DMUs that had been purchased to run the daily commuter services between Minehead and Taunton.

By May 1976 the railway was operating a steam service four times each day on the Minehead-Blue Anchor section of the branch, with the intention of operating a diesel service of not fewer than four trains a day between Minehead and Taunton using the two Park Royal two-car sets acquired from BR, this being subject to completion of a running powers agreement with British Rail. The Directors hoped that such a scheme would prove popular with commuters, shoppers, schoolchildren and others wanting to travel to Taunton, in preference to the bus service, which took longer and was often delayed on the busy local roads.

By 1978 the WSR was establishing itself as a working railway, providing an alternative to the road transport difficulties faced in West Somerset and conveying local people and holidaymakers through the attractive scenery of this part of England, which was recognised as an area of great natural beauty that includes the Quantock and Brendon Hills and the West Somerset coast. The well-subscribed share issue of 1976, taken up eagerly by locals as well as railway enthusiasts, had provided the funding for extending the operation, enabling the company to increase its passenger journeys by 8% between 1976 and 1977 and to double the traffic on the six-days-a-week shoppers' service. Reaching Taunton and the BR main line was still a priority, thus making the WSR the longest privately operated railway in Britain with a route of 25 miles, but the capital costs of this connection, including the annual rent for running over the final 2½ miles on BR metals, were considerable, although funding had allowed the station at Bishops Lydeard to be restored, and two of the railway's GWR '55XX' 2-6-2Ts were there awaiting restoration, while the other 'Prairie', No 4561, was being stripped down at Minehead in the company of LB&SCR 'Terrier' *Knowle*.

As well as the two Park Royal DMUs, which in 1978 ran the all-year-round

A DMU set with car 51859 at the head pauses at Washford on 28 July 1999, forming the 1305 Bishops Lydeard-Minehead duty. *John Stretton*

No 4277 ready to return a special charter train to Minehead on 13 July 1996. *John Stretton*

service, the WSR had GWR 0-6-0PT No 6412 and two 'Super Bagnalls', but the immediate need was for further operational steam locos to share the work. Restoration was proceeding on the first of the railway's three GWR 'Prairie' tanks (No 4561 mentioned above) and the Diesel & Electric Group's 'Hymek' No D7017, as well as the S&D Railway Museum Trust's 2-8-0 No 88. A further appeal to raise £60,000 to enable the railway to reach Taunton and to repay the loan from Somerset County Council was therefore launched.

By 1981 the WSR was well and truly established, with its headquarters and main station at Minehead and a regular service of diesel and steam trains operating to Bishops Lydeard (20 miles), with a connecting bus service to nearby Taunton.

The locomotive stock at that time consisted of LB&SCR Class 'A1X' 0-6-0T No 78, built in 1880, S&DJR 7F 2-8-0 No 88 of 1925, GWR locos '4500' Class 2-6-2T No 4561 (1924), '4575' Class 2-6-2T No 5542 (1928) and '6400' Class 0-6-0PT No 6412 (1934), and BR locos Class 35 No D7017 (1962), Class 07 0-6-0 diesel-electric shunter D2994 (1962), and Class 14 0-6-0 diesel-hydraulic No D9526 (1964)

Industrial locomotives included three 0-6-0STs, No S3 *Portbury*, built by Avonside in 1917, No 2994 *Vulcan* (Bagnall, 1950) and No 2996 *Victor* (Bagnall, 1951); the last two had been acquired at a 'bargain price' from the British Leyland Motor Corporation at Longbridge, Birmingham. There were also 0-4-0STs Nos 2473 (Bagnall, 1932) and 1163 *Whitehead* (Peckett, 1908), 0-6-0ST No 3437 *Isabel* (Hawthorn Leslie, 1919), 0-4-0ST No 1788 *Kilmersdon* (Peckett, 1929), and two Ruston 4WDMs from 1937 and 1941.

Stock in use included six ex-BR Mk 1 coaches, two ex-BR suburban coaches, four ex-GWR camping coaches, six ex-BR Pullman cars, one ex-LNER coach, two ex-SR 'Ironclad' coaches, two Park Royal two-car DMUs, one ex-GWR Hawksworth coach, one ex-LMS parcels van, and more than 20 freight vehicles.

No 7820 *Dinmore Manor* stands at Bishops Lydeard, surrounded by holidaymakers, on 17 July 1999, ready to leave with the 16.05 train to Minehead. *John Stretton*

At that time the WSR timetable showed that the journey time from Taunton to Watchet was 1 hour (compared with 50 minutes in 1862), though about 20-25 minutes of this was accounted for by the bus service between Bishops Lydeard and the BR station at Taunton (about 5 miles).

A new turntable installed at Minehead station in 2008 allows visiting steam locomotives on charter trains to be serviced and turned before returning to the national network. It is also used extensively during gala days and for other special events.

2011 saw the opening of the new Waiting Room at Stogumber station, which complements the highly praised Refreshment Room at the tiny rural station near the picturesque village that bears its name.

The station at the eastern end of the line, Bishops Lydeard, 4 miles from Taunton, now boasts a Gauge Museum, housing many exhibits of local interest, while the 'Whistle Stop Café' and station shop cater for those in need of sustenance or retail therapy.

Bibliography

Body, G. *An Illustrated History of Preserved Railways* (Moorland)
BR Eastern Region Cavalcade Reflections (1975, BR ER)
Butcher, A. C. *Railways Restored: Preserved Locomotives* (Ian Allan)
Coffin, R. *Mainline Steam in the 70s* (1974, 6000 Locomotive Association)
Crombleholme, R. *Steam 73: The ARPS Year Book and Steam Guide* (Haraton Ltd)
Eatwell, D. & Cooper-Smith, J. H. *Return to Steam* (1978, Batsford)
Fox, P. & Hall, P. *Preserved Locomotives of British Railways* (Platform 5)
Kennedy, R. *Ian Allan's 50 Years of Railways* (1992, BCA)
Nabarro, Sir G. *Steam Nostalgia* (1972, Routledge & Kegan Paul)
Railway World *Railways Restored* (1981, Ian Allan)
Ransom, P. J. G. *Railways Revived* (1973, Faber & Faber)
Sharman, Bill *Main Line Steam: 25 Glorious Years of Preservation* (1997, Atlantic)
Skelton, P. J. C. *Mainline Steam into the 1980s* (1984, Jane's Publishing Co Ltd)
Urie S15 Preservation Group *The Barry List, 2nd and 6th Editions* (1975 and 1981)

The NOSTALGIA *Collection*

A growing range of titles from both the Silver Link and Past & Present imprints.
The range includes both individual or 'stand alone' titles and series that provide for collections
based on various subject themes. Examples appear below:

THE FALL AND RISE of
British Railways
STEAM
John Stretton & Peter Townsend

The last steam locomotive built for British Railways, aptly named Evening Star, was
outshopped from Swindon Works in 1960, and amazingly the last steam locomotives
were withdrawn from service in August 1968! This decline from the mid-1950s forms
the first part of this book, as hundreds upon hundreds of locomotives were sent to
the breaker's yards.

The scrap yards are the sombre location of the second section, which looks at
these 'abattoirs of steam', where the vast majority of locomotives were despatched
by the cutter's torch all too rapidly. However, among the scenes of devastation
something remarkable was happening. Enthusiasts noticed that at one yard, old
wagons were being cut up but locomotives were not.

This was the remarkable yard of Dai Woodham at Barry Docks in South
Wales – locomotives were going to Dai, but not to die! Thanks in large part to this remarkable man we are able to move to our third section, the preservation years, when locomotives
were reserved, then purchased (often gradually) and eventually moved to fledgling preserved
lines all over the country to be restored.

Having been banned seemingly for ever, steam eventually returned to the main line, and
the book concludes with a look at today's thriving heritage railway scene, with more than 8
million visitors a year – a fall and rise indeed!

276 x 213mm 160pp c320 b&w and colour illustrations
ISBN: 978 1 85794 330 6   Hardback £30.00

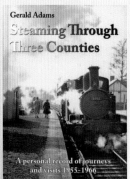

STEAMING THROUGH THREE COUNTIES
A personal record of journeys and visits 1955-1966
Gerald Adams

A tribute to the memory of lifelong railway enthusiast and photographer, the
late Gerald Adams, and to the memory of the steam age, this book contains
more than 280 photographs, selected and captioned by Gerald. The pictures
span the years 1955 to 1966, that momentous final decade when steam was
disappearing almost faster than it could be recorded. The area covered by the
photographs reflects where Gerald lived during that period, first Birmingham,
then Gloucester.

As a result, he planned the book to include principally the 'Cathedral
Counties' of Gloucestershire, Herefordshire and Worcestershire, with slight
excursions across the county boundaries. Some pictures were taken on journeys
by service trains, some were rail tours, and some were just platform-end
sojourns, recording the passing scene.

The pictures are arranged chronologically, from Kings Norton in
March 1955 to a Stephenson Locomotive Society 'Pannier Tank Farewell' rail
tour in September 1966. Timetables of 20 of the journeys and specials are also included.
From Craven Arms and Birmingham, Hereford and Honeybourne, Bristol and Swindon,
here is a feast of Western and London Midland Region steam at work in three of England's
most picturesque counties.

238 x 172mm 160pp c300 b&w illustrations
ISBN: 978 1 85794 350 4   Hardback £25.00

Souvenir Guide

WELCOME

The West Somerset Railway is Britain's longest standard gauge heritage railway and carries more than 200,000 passengers per year, making it one of Somerset's most popular tourist attractions. Passenger trains run during most months of the year, with services from early February to early December. In addition to offering an 80-minute 'pink knuckle' ride through the Quantock Hills and along the Exmoor Coast, the Railway has also developed a number of combined packages with other local attractions including Dunster Castle and Hestercombe Gardens, as well as day trips around Exmoor and exploring the remains of the old West Somerset Mineral Railway. Much more information can be obtained by ringing 01643 704996 or viewing the Company website at www.west-somerset-railway.co.uk.

Time Line

1856-1862
West Somerset Railway constructed between Norton Fitzwarren and Watchet

1874
Line extended to Minehead

1882
Line converted from broad gauge to standard gauge

1934
Final expansion occurs

1948
Railways nationalised

1971
Minehead branch closed by British Rail

1976
First WSR trains begin running between Minehead and Blue Anchor

1979
Train operations reach full length of line between Minehead and Bishops Lydeard

2012
150th Anniversary

AN OUTLINE OF THE WEST SOMERSET LINE

Wealthy Victorians were as a whole an enterprising group of people and, once railways had proved themselves to be an invaluable way of moving goods and people and increasing trade, it was felt that no self-respecting town that wished to prosper could afford not to be linked to the growing national network. One such place was the Bristol Channel harbour town of Watchet.

Shipping had traded in and out of Watchet for more than 1,000 years before the first trains on the West Somerset Mineral Railway, built to give an outlet for the iron ore being mined in the Brendon Hills, reached the harbour. The ore went to the furnaces of South Wales, hence the WSMR was backed by the Ebbw Vale Company. It did also run passenger trains but, as the line went up into the hills rather than towards Taunton and the main-line network, its usefulness for general trade was limited.

The West Somerset Railway was therefore promoted to run from Norton Fitzwarren Junction, just west of Taunton on the Bristol & Exeter Railway main line through the Quantock Hills to Watchet. Recognising that having a famous engineer linked to the project would help to attract local and financial support, the promoters approached Isambard Kingdom Brunel, whose practice agreed to survey and oversee the building of the WSR. In reality, in 1856 Brunel himself

'The Beeching axe'

When in 1962 Dr Richard Beeching produced his report 'The Reshaping of British Railways', the Minehead line was earmarked for closure.

It was, however, a marginal case. Whereas the other branch lines from Taunton to Chard (closed 1962), Yeovil (closed 1964) and Barnstaple (closed 1966) went fairly quickly, the Minehead made money in the summer and lost it in the winter.

was fully occupied with the Saltash railway bridge and his ship *Great Eastern*, so the work was delegated to one of his assistants, Mr Burke. Able to draw on three decades of building lines, Burke followed the usual practice when crossing a range of hills, following one watercourse to the summit and another on the way down. The hardest and most thankless task was that of the agent who had to negotiate land purchase with local landowners, who looked to gain the maximum financial advantage from the railway promoters with the least inconvenience to themselves. Construction began with the large cutting near the site of Crowcombe Heathfield (which gave a reserve store of waste soil and stone to build embankments as required elsewhere), and by 1862 the line was complete.

In 1874 the line was extended to Minehead as part of a wider scheme to convert a generally moribund harbour town into a resort for the rapidly growing popularity of seaside holidays. This was done by a nominally independent company, the Minehead Railway, and architecturally there are two obvious legacies: first, the fact that Watchet's station building still stands at right-angles to the

track from its days as a terminus, and second, two distinct designs of station buildings.

Both lines were built to the same gauge as the Bristol & Exeter, Brunel's 'broad' gauge of 7ft 0¼in – but converted to standard gauge in 1882 – and were effectively worked by the B&E from the start. In turn the B&E was bought out by the Great Western Railway, under whose ownership facilities and platform lengths at stations were expanded to cope with growing numbers of passengers. In 1948 the railways were nationalised and the line became part of British Railways.

Local all-year-round traffic had begun a decline in the 1920s and '30s as the rural bus, then the private car, ate into business. The buses could go through villages while stations such as Crowcombe Heathfield and Stogumber were a good distance from local communities, and the car offered even more flexibility. Holiday traffic, however, continued to develop, reaching a peak in the 1950s and seeing Butlins open a holiday centre at Minehead in the late 1960s. When the County Council moved all of the schools traffic to the roads as the 1970s dawned, the loss of this year-round income precipitated closure and the line succumbed at

Top right: North Hill dominates the skyline of Minehead, representing the point where Exmoor comes down to the Bristol Channel, with the town extending part way up its slopes. The modernistic pavilion building is part of the Butlins Holiday Centre from where many holidaymakers come to enjoy a day out on the Railway and in the surrounding area. *Don Bishop*

Left: Locomotive No 9351 is an interesting WSR creation, a steam locomotive designed by the Great Western Railway in the 1930s but not actually built by the GWR. The West Somerset converted a scrap-condition 'Large Prairie' tank engine No 5193 to produce this 'Small Boilered Mogul', and seven decades after the original design it has proved to be an excellent engine. *Don Bishop*

Great Western 'auto-trains' never operated on the Minehead line in GWR or British Railways days, being deployed on less heavily used branch lines, but they have proved very popular attractions during Enthusiast Gala events. *WSR Collection*

the start of 1971. Bearing in mind the changing attitudes towards railways in the mid to late 1970s, had the line lasted just a few more years it would probably not have closed. Much reduction had already taken place, however, with goods yards and other track lifted and buildings closed and demolished. Survival would likely have meant a single-line basic railway, with 'bus shelters' on platforms and possibly a relocated terminus at Minehead.

Taunton – so near and yet so far...

The eventual target was to run commuter trains to Taunton, but now a major problem emerged.

When bus services were being introduced in the West of England, many were originally operated by the Great Western Railway, and a legacy of this was that many drivers employed by the Western National company were members of the National Union of Railwaymen, and the WSR trains were viewed as potentially taking business from the then route 218 between Taunton and Minehead. The junction at Norton Fitzwarren and access to Taunton station were 'blacked', and the existing year-round West Somerset trains were confined to running through the smaller towns and villages along the way. Reduced-price travel was available for local residents, but even so usage of winter trains fell away, with the county town and its station being so near and yet so far.

THE RE-OPENING OF THE LINE

During the long time it took to close the Minehead line, plans had been laid to re-open it as a private railway. At the time there were various schemes, which envisaged breaking away from the steam-worked tourist railway model pioneered by the Talyllyn in 1951 and working commuter services all year round with diesel railcar trains augmented by steam trains in the summer. The WSR was intended to follow this pattern.

However, it was five years before the new Company could run its first train. During that time volunteers from the West Somerset Railway Association had done much to clear plant growth along the route and begin to re-fettle track and buildings. One major train movement had happened in that time when the 'Coronation' Class 'Pacific' *Duchess of Hamilton* was towed along the branch en route from Butlins Minehead to the National Railway Museum. Hauled by Class 25 diesel No 25059, the movement of this heavy locomotive demonstrated that the track, bridges and culverts were inherently sound.

The first train ran between Minehead and Blue Anchor, flagged away by Lord Montague of Beaulieu, on 28 March 1976, and from then on the expansion of services proceeded at a rapid pace, with Bishops Lydeard formally becoming the southern terminus on 9 June 1979.

The rapid expansion of the journey to the point where the West Somerset was, and still is, the longest standard gauge 'heritage' line in Britain had strained resources and it was becoming apparent that some of the motive power was struggling.

DARK DAYS

By the start of the 1980s the Company was to all intents and purposes flat broke and approaching closure with virtually no operational motive power. From that point the only possibilities were a winding-up or a fight-back led by a group determined that the West Somerset could be turned round. Nearly all the paid staff were made redundant, the winter services were ended and simpler timetables devised that could be operated with existing resources. This included only one daily round trip by steam over the whole of the line, running in the morning, with one or two Minehead-Williton round trips in the afternoon. It was also at this time that the Taunton area was resignalled with colour lights, replacing the time-honoured semaphores, and as part of this the old separate line from Norton Fitzwarren to Taunton station was lifted, with new signalling being installed on and under the trackbed. That seriously reduced any future chances of WSR trains reaching Taunton, but at the time it was understandable that British Rail was expecting that the West Somerset would not be in business to use the line. Through the first five years of the 1980s things remained parlous.

HARD WORK, SUPPORT AND ENTHUSIASM BRINGS BRIGHTER DAYS

Somerset County Council in particular was very supportive, many of the laid-off paid staff stayed on as volunteers, and this general will and drive to succeed was starting to pay off.

In 1986 for the first time it was possible to hire a steam locomotive from elsewhere (Great Western 'Small Prairie' No 5572 from Didcot), and in 1987 Minehead locomotive department completed the overhaul of Somerset & Dorset Joint Railway No 53808 (now No 88), which gave the Railway an engine capable of attracting crowds and pulling the trains they were on. In 1989 the last steam engine to be built for British Railways, 9F 2-10-0 No 92220 *Evening Star*, was hired for a year and visitors flocked to the Railway as never before. Other engines were also being brought to the line and restored, and with that came greater reliability, more steam mileage and more passengers. In 1996 the Railway held its first Spring Steam Gala, and with each year more achievements were racked up including successfully dealing with stone trains for Minehead sea defence work and 'Railway of the Year' awards.

Today the West Somerset Railway is firmly established as a major attraction in South West England, carrying more than 200,000 passengers each year. There is a paid staff of more than 50 and some 900 volunteers involved in all aspects of keeping the trains running (and the Railway as a whole presenting its best aspect to visitors).

'Will Something Run?'

The steam services depended largely in the early years on two industrial engines, *Victor* and *Vulcan*. Built by Bagnall of Stafford for steelworks use in Wales, they had subsequently gone to Austin Motors at Longbridge, from where they were purchased by the infant WSR. As supremely powerful industrial shunters they may well have been suited to short steam trips for holidaymakers, but a 40-mile round trip with hard climbing and a route that twisted and turned through the hills was not their forte. Timekeeping and reliability was poor, and as the second-hand diesel railcars also suffered from the high mileage, service reliability plummeted to the point where a local joke held that WSR stood for 'Will Something Run?'. To this must be added a complicated early timetable leaflet, which the public found hard to understand.

Class 158 diesel units would be ideal candidates for any regular services between the main-line network and Minehead if these were to come about. In the meantime they sometimes appear at Bishops Lydeard on shuttles from Taunton during special events.
Claire Rickson

Railway terms

Straight away some railway terms need to be clarified. On most railways 'up' trains were those that headed for London and 'down' those that headed away from the capital. Thus, if you were travelling from Paddington to Minehead anything to the left of the direction of travel was on the 'down side', while anything to the right was on the 'up side'. From Minehead towards Paddington, the 'up side' was on the left and the 'down side' on the right. It is these terms that this Guide Book uses; hopefully things will become clearer as your journey proceeds. If in doubt, ask one of the on-train staff – it will be an easier question for them to answer than some that they are asked!

Enthusiast Galas bring large numbers of passengers, photographers and visitors to the WSR, and here a demonstration 'heritage' freight train passes a shuttle-service Class 158 unit at Bishops Lydeard station. *Claire Rickson*

Bishops Lydeard remains the usual southern terminus for most WSR services. Having spent the first 109 years of its existence as a typical wayside branch-line station on the edge of the village it served, it has inevitably had to be modified for its new role. Bus services between Taunton and Minehead pass through the station area on days when the WSR trains are running and there is a good-sized car park for intending passengers. By whatever route you arrive, access to the platforms is via a ramp by the signal box, which brings you to the building that now contains the booking office, the well-stocked model and souvenir shop and the Whistle Stop café. For ease of access most trains leave from this platform, which was once the one for 'up' trains, and which was extended in the 1990s to cope with longer trains and excursions from the national network.

Over on Platform 1 the original station building is now used as offices for the West Somerset Railway Association and a mess room for the station staff. The former goods shed is now the Gauge Museum, housing a collection of artefacts from former railway lines in South West England and at least one large item of historic rolling stock. A replica of Powderham signal box shows the workings of a small box in the days of steam. There is a large model railway

BISHOPS LYDEARD

Station notes

Opened: 1862
Closed: 1971
Reopened: 1979
Ownership:
    West Somerset Railway
    Great Western Railway
    British Railways
    West Somerset Railway
Platforms: Two
Signal box: Yes
Toilets: Yes (RADAR)
Cafe: Yes

DISABLED PARKING

Shop: Yes
Platform access: Easy access shallow ramp to platform

on the upper floor, which operates on days when enough volunteer labour is available. In between the Gauge Museum and the station building is the club room of the Taunton Model Group, which is usually open to the public on Gala days and home to some of the best railway modelling in the country.

Bishops Lydeard itself is a large dormitory village for Taunton, but by walking up Station Road, through Gore Square and towards the impressive church you can see and enjoy the older parts. The old Mill is open during the summer months, and there are a number of village shops, including a chemist, and two pubs.

BISHOPS LYDEARD TO NORTON FITZWARREN

This section of track only sees passenger trains on special occasions such as Galas and during the annual Steam Fayre. As we head away from Bishops Lydeard station the loco compound is on the up side followed by the Cotford carriage sidings. In recent years a turning triangle of track has been built, which can be seen on the down side as the train passes the platform constructed for use when the show area at WSRA Fields is being utilised. The triangle uses a section of the former Taunton-Barnstaple line running parallel to the West of England main line, but the West Somerset has no plans to open any more.

Through trains from the main-line network appear regularly on the West Somerset, and here we see 'A1' Class 'Pacific' No 60163 *Tornado* drawing the crowds at Bishops Lydeard as it heads towards Minehead. *Brian Pibworth*

The climate of Taunton Deane and West Somerset is very mild, and pictures of trains in frost and snow are not easy to obtain. Here GWR 'Small Prairie' is running round its train at Bishops Lydeard in the post-Christmas services period. *Claire Rickson*

BISHOPS LYDEARD TO CROWCOMBE HEATHFIELD

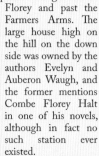

Great Western '2884' Class heavy freight locomotive No 3850 is approaching the top of the climb from Bishops Lydeard and arriving at the highest point of the line at Crowcombe Heathfield. The locomotive is owned by Dinmore Manor Locomotive Ltd.
Alan Tupman

Assuming that you are travelling on a regular service train to Minehead, your train will leave Bishops Lydeard heading north under the road bridge that takes traffic to Ash Priors and Halse. As it gets under way it passes between the Greenway housing estate on the down side and the grounds of Dunkirk House on the up; the latter is a British Legion retirement home for ex-servicemen and their widows. Passing through Eastcombe cutting and over Whiskey Trail foot crossing (so named by United States servicemen who used it en route to the village pubs during the Second World War), trains start the climb into the Quantock Hills.

If you are travelling in the front or rear part of a diesel railcar, the view ahead reveals how the line climbs and twists on its way through this Area of Outstanding Natural Beauty. From the windows of a steam train the view is of a constantly changing series of wide views and small scenes. The Taunton-Minehead A358 road is crossed twice in quick succession as the train passes through Combe Florey and past the Farmers Arms. The large house high on the hill on the down side was owned by the authors Evelyn and Auberon Waugh, and the former mentions Combe Florey Halt in one of his novels, although in fact no such station ever existed.

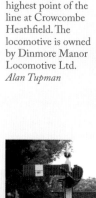

The train now passes through a mixture of wooded countryside and pasture. Along this stretch and for most of the way to Williton you may be lucky enough to see some of the local wildlife. The most common sight is the gaudy plumage of cock pheasants (the hens are far harder to spot), while in the air there is a very good chance of seeing a buzzard, quite often being mobbed by wary rooks or other crows. Buzzards also sometimes sit on lineside fence-posts, providing the opportunity to observe these large birds of prey close up. Red kites are just beginning to reappear in the area after an absence of many years. The embankments of the line betray the presence of rabbits, and they too can often be seen in the fields. It is not unknown to see deer, but they are wary and move very quickly into cover when disturbed.

Having been climbing since leaving Bishops Lydeard, the train now enters a long deep cutting that takes it past the highest point of the line and under a high road bridge before rolling into Crowcombe Heathfield station.

CROWCOMBE HEATHFIELD

This is the most remote station on the line, reflected in the various names it has carried over the years. In part this was due to the Great Western Railway being ultra-cautious about any confusion that might be suffered by passengers regarding which train or line they should be on. That therefore ruled out Heathfield (there was already one on the Exe Valley line), or the

STATION NOTES

Opened: 1862
Closed: 1971
Reopened: 1979
Ownership:
    West Somerset Railway
    Great Western Railway
    British Railways
    West Somerset Railway

Platforms: Two
Signal box: Yes
Toilets: Yes
Cafe: Yes
Shop: No
Platform access: Grassed area
    level to platform

Cycles are carried in the guards vans of the 1950s coaching stock of the Railway. Here a large group of cyclists who have enjoyed the quiet roads in the Quantock Hills await a train at Crowcombe Heathfield. *All Tim Stanger*

In the first of these views of contrasting trains and weather at Crowcombe Heathfield, GWR No 1450 heads a two-coach 'auto-train'. The snow-covered winter scene is picturesque, but does not seem to have brought many visitors. Finally, a 'Warship' Class diesel-hydraulic double-heads a down train with No 9351. *Steve Richardson/Tim Stanger (2)*

reasonably nearby Lydeard St Lawrence (confusion with Bishops Lydeard being feared). For quite a bit of its history the station was simply Crowcombe, but that village is more than 2 miles away, and many of the inhabitants found Stogumber station just as convenient for their journeys.

Be all that as it may, the station is a charming spot in itself and its remoteness has made it a favourite with film and TV companies as a country station location. Among its big-screen appearances are *The Land Girls* and the Beatles film *A Hard Day's Night*.

Having been reduced to a single track during the run-down by BR, the West Somerset has reinstated the signal box (the wooden part is from a GWR box in South Wales) and the signalling, and it is now an important passing point for trains at busier times. Over the years the Station Masters and their helpers have created award-winning surroundings and installed a toilet for disabled passengers, then in 2010 the booking office was brought back into use. Light refreshments are usually available. At the Minehead end of the down-side platform there is a display of trackwork, including an example of broad gauge track, while on the other side of the line an embankment marks the site of a siding formerly used for loading stone from local quarries into trains. The station is a popular one for walkers who wish to explore the Quantock Hills.

CROWCOMBE HEATHFIELD TO STOGUMBER

Leaving Crowcombe Heathfield, the line begins a long descent to Williton, passing the former Station Master's house on the up side just before the train passes under another road bridge. Shortly after this it passes over the level crossing at Roebuck Gate. This section of the route is another mixture of pastureland and woods, with some distant views of Exmoor appearing on the down side. The line passes over another level crossing at Leigh Woods, and over another road bridge as it enters Stogumber station.

Top: An evocative view of the West Somerset Railway in the Quantock Hills as GWR 'Small Prairie' No 5542 heads a train near Cotford Bridge. *Sam Burton*

Centre: Super power to spare as Great Western 'King' Class No 6024 *King Edward I* double-heads with an LMS 'Black 5' on a down train arriving at Crowcombe Heathfield. *Tim Stanger*

Bottom: Not a daily scene on the WSR, but here we see a London & South Western Railway Beattie well tank engine dating from the 1870s trundling a short demonstration freight train through the Quantocks. The locomotive was hired from the Bodmin & Wenford Railway for a steam gala event. *Martin Southwood*

STATION NOTES

Opened: 1862
Closed: 1971
Reopened: 1978
Ownership:
   West Somerset Railway
   Great Western Railway
   British Railways
   West Somerset Railway
Platforms: One
Signal box: No
Toilets: Yes
Cafe: Yes
Shop: No
Platform access: Too narrow – steep ramp to platform

STOGUMBER

The station layout here is very peculiar, and passengers on the up side of the train have been known to wonder where the platform is, while those on the down have been looking for the main building. The reason for the separation is that the station is cut into a hillside and the slope can be best appreciated by looking over the platform fence and seeing how far below is the former Railway Inn (now a private house). The former goods yard area, cleared during the line's run-down, is now an inviting picnic garden, and the station sells refreshments including cream teas. Tickets can also be purchased.

Stogumber village is not visible from the station, as it lies about a mile away over a ridge of hills on the down side. The walk is very enjoyable along a fairly quiet road, and the village pub, 'The White Horse', is open all day. There was once a brewery in the village, but this closed in the 1930s.

This page and opposite top: These two pictures show the unusual layout of Stogumber station's hillside location. 'Small Prairie' No 5553 restarts an up train on the climb towards Crowcombe Heathfield while a diesel multiple unit is rather overshadowed by the splendid garden and picnic area. Does a cream tea at this location look tempting? They are served in the summer between May and October. *Tim Stanger/Alan Turner*

STATION FACT

For many years the late Harry Horne had a good claim to the title of 'world's oldest station master', greeting passengers at Stogumber until his death in his tenth decade. After his passing his widow Iris continued as station master until just before her own death. Harry features in the book *Tales of the Old Railwaymen.*

STOGUMBER TO WILLITON

The train continues its descent until Woolston Moor, where the countryside opens out as the Quantocks reach the Bristol Channel. The line passes under two bridges in quick succession and past a railwayside cottage as the hamlet of Sampford Brett is passed on the down side. Another short cutting takes the line to the bridge over the A358 road and along an embankment between Castle Hill and the wooded banks of the Doniford stream. The Doniford passes under the line just before the train runs under the road carrying the A39 Bridgwater-Minehead road and arrives at Williton station.

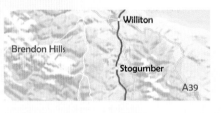

One of the most photographed locations on the WSR is Castle Hill near Williton, where the line passes over the A358 Williton-Taunton road. Here 'Small Prairie' No 5553 is starting the steady climb towards Stogumber and Crowcombe. *Alan Turner*

WILLITON

STATION NOTES

Opened: 1862
Closed: 1971
Reopened: 1976
Ownership:
West Somerset Railway
Great Western Railway
British Railways
West Somerset Railway
Platforms: Two
Signal box: Yes
Toilets: No
Cafe: Yes
Shop: No
Platform access: Narrow – shallow ramp to platform

The station stands on the edge of Williton and boasts a good deal of railway interest. It is another passing station, and the train movements are controlled by the only surviving Bristol & Exeter Railway signal box, dating from the 1860s. There is also a legacy of the line's broad gauge origins in the form of the wider than normal gap between the two running lines. The station is able to offer refreshments, while on the up side the small former waiting room is a shop that raises money for station maintenance.

Middle right: The footbridge at Williton station was once located at Trowbridge. Erected at its new home in 2010 after many years of fund-raising, it will gain a roof and lighting when funds permit. Here it frames Great Northern Railway 'N2' Class No 1744 during the 2011 Autumn Steam Gala. *Sam Burton*

Bottom right: Also during the 2011 Autumn Steam Gala, GWR heavy freight engine No 3850 (owned by Dinmore Manor Locomotive Ltd and based on the West Somerset) arrives with a down train heading towards Minehead. (Yes, the weather really was this good in October 2011!) *Dave Reynolds*

During the history of the modern WSR much has happened on the wider site, and it is now a major engineering base. In 2011 work began on erecting a new footbridge at the station, fulfilling a long-standing desire of the former Station Master Chris van den Arend, who died at the end of 2010; once completed the bridge was officially returned to use on 16 July 2011.

The Diesel & Electric Preservation Group came to the West Somerset in the early years and loyally supported the project through the dark days of the early 1980s. Its first base was in the former goods shed, but as its fleet of vintage diesel locomotives has grown it has built a large modern depot and workshop, while a Diesel Locomotive Heritage Centre has been set up in the Goods Shed. This is

Left: 'King Arthur' Class No 30777 *Sir Lamiel* makes a spectacular departure from Williton with an up train towards Bishops Lydeard. The locomotive spent the spring of 2011 on hire to the West Somerset Railway and is the only surviving example of this class of express locomotives built for the Southern Railway. *WSR Collection*

open on most weekends when trains are running and during special events on the Railway. Beyond the DEPG base is another large building. This was once part of the Great Western Railway Works at Swindon, but was presented to the West Somerset by Tarmac Ltd. Since re-erection on its present site it has been fitted out as a workshop and is now run by West Somerset Restoration, which overhauls locomotives, rolling stock and other machinery, both for the West Somerset and for other groups and private owners. This is not generally open to the public.

Williton itself is one of those large villages that seems more like a small town. The centre is around 15 minutes' walk from the station, and once there you will find a small shopping centre with two banks, two supermarkets, a post office and newsagent, and a variety of smaller independent retailers. It is another 10 minutes on to the Bakelite Museum, which houses an amazing array of artefacts made from this pioneering plastic material, ranging from the expected telephones and radios through to a caravan. For the hungry and thirsty there are four pubs and an Indian restaurant.

Bottom left: The large restoration shed at the Minehead end of Williton station was once part of the Great Western Railway workshops at Swindon. Today it is home to West Somerset Restorations and the West Somerset Steam Railway Trust, and here we see GWR 'Modified Hall' No 6960 *Raveningham Hall* undergoing heavy overhaul. This locomotive returned to passenger working at the 2011 Winter Steam Festival. *Justin Kerr-Peterson*

DONIFORD HALT

Built by the current WSR utilising a platform recovered from Montacute on the Taunton – Yeovil branch (closed in 1964) and a corrugated iron pagoda shelter from Cove on the Exe Valley line (closed in 1963). Situated by the bridge which carries the Doniford –Watchet road over the line most of the passengers who use the Halt are staying at the nearby Haven Holiday Centre. It is what is known in railway terms as a "request stop" which means that intending travellers need to signal for the train to stop and those wishing to alight there need to inform the guard or travelling ticket inspector in good time.

Right: A visiting 'Black 5' locomotive heads a train towards Bishops Lydeard along the cliff-top section at Doniford. When the line was originally built it was nearly 100 yards inland at this point, reflecting the problems of protecting the line for the future against coastal erosion and the tide range of the Bristol Channel.
Sam Burton

WILLITON TO WATCHET
(PASSING THROUGH DONIFORD HALT)

Leaving Williton the train curves away over a road and heads for the coast of the Bristol Channel, which can be seen ahead from the up side of the train. As it nears the sea the line turns again, and Doniford Halt is reached.

Once past the Halt the train is running along the cliff tops on a section where coastal erosion is constantly monitored. After a short distance Helwell Bay caravan site is on the up side, with new housing on the down.

The train passes through another cutting and runs into Watchet. As it does so the reason for the construction of the original line cannot be missed on the up side – the harbour.

HALT NOTES

Opened: 1987
Ownership:
 West Somerset Railway
Platforms: One
Signal box: No
Toilets: No
Cafe: No
Shop: No
Platform access: Very difficult – small uneven gravel path leads down from road embankment with gated entrance (and no car parking)

WATCHET

The station has a long single platform with the station building at right-angles to the single track, housing the booking office and a shop area together with the station's toilets. The former goods shed is now out of railway ownership, as is the footbridge, and is used as a Boat Museum given over to small craft used by the folk who made at least some of their living from the Bristol Channel.

STATION NOTES

Opened: 1862
Closed: 1971
Reopened: 1976
Ownership:
  West Somerset Railway
  Great Western Railway
  British Railways
  West Somerset Railway
Platforms: Two
Signal box: No
Toilets: Yes
Cafe: No
Shop: Yes
Platform access: Easy – level access to platform

Walking from Watchet station immediately puts you in the middle of the small town. The large building opposite the station is the former cinema, and beyond that is the Council Chambers and the main street, which has a variety of small local shops (some of which still observe an early closing day on Wednesday afternoons). Once again there are a number of pubs, cafés and restaurants. The Town Museum houses a wide variety of displays reflecting Watchet's long history, including a section given over to the West Somerset Mineral Railway, whose former station stands at right-angles to the road beyond the 'Star Inn' and opposite the west quay, where once the iron ore was loaded from the Mineral Railway into ships for the voyage to the furnaces of South Wales

Above: The long platform at Watchet station curves towards Bishops Lydeard, the Goviers Lane exit from the station on to the Quay, and the old harbour, which is now a Marina. *Sam Burton*

Left: This picture demonstrates how the station building at Watchet was originally built as a terminus, standing at right-angles to the track and with the embankment at the rear cut away to make room for it. *Sam Burton*

Right: This nocturnal picture again shows Watchet's station building standing at right-angles to the running line, reflecting the station's original status as a terminus between 1862 and 1874. *Keith Smith*

Bottom right: No 7828 (originally *Odney Manor* but temporarily renamed *Norton Manor 40 Commando*) arrives with a down train during the 2011 Autumn Steam Gala. *Julian Moore*

WATCHET HARBOUR

The last commercial traffic used the port of Watchet in the 1990s, since when the harbour has become a marina and a source of business for the regeneration of the town as a whole. Trains once ran on to the quays for loading; one of the last commercial cargoes to be carried was esparto grass from Spain, which was used in the local Watchet Paper Mill and also taken by rail to the mill at Hele and Bradninch on the main line between Taunton and Exeter.

WATCHET TO WASHFORD

The exit from Watchet on to what was originally the Minehead Railway is convoluted and confined. The station is left in a cutting on a curve

that opens out as the train runs on to the bridge over the trackbed of the former Mineral Railway. It then enters another curve that takes the line to a point where it runs parallel to the Mineral Railway trackbed (now a popular footpath) and the Washford River. The train is also now climbing once again through more arable land, with the Quantocks as the backdrop on the up side and the nearer view dominated by the masts of the former radio station, which now houses the Tropiquaria Animal Centre. As the train approaches Washford the old Mineral Railway embankment swings away behind the playing fields and the climb ends as the station is reached.

WASHFORD

This is the first of the Minehead Railway stations and the architecture of the main building is very different from those between Bishops Lydeard and Watchet. Today it houses the Museum of the Somerset & Dorset Railway Trust, which came to the WSR as the line was re-opening and established its base here. Before closure the site had been reduced to a single running line, so all the sidings, the shed and workshop, and the other buildings have been put in place by SDRT volunteers. There is a sales counter in the Museum that sells the Trust's own publications and a good selection of the many publications about the Somerset & Dorset line that have appeared over the years. The S&D itself ran from Bath to Bournemouth with branches to Bridgwater, Burnham-on-Sea and Wells, and finally closed as a through route in 1966.

The 'Washford Inn' stands right beside the station and offers food and drink, and a garden with a play area. Cleeve Abbey lies approximately 10 minutes away along a signposted route through to the village. Now in the care of English Heritage, the main church building has gone but the outbuildings are in fine condition and offer a good view of monastic life. Further along Abbey Road, at a road junction, is the 'White Horse Inn', another pub with food and drink and a large garden across the road. The left-hand road crosses the Mineral Railway trackbed at Torre level crossing, and a little further along is Torre Cider Farm. This is open to the public to explain how cider is made, and the product can be sampled (treat it with respect!) and purchased.

STATION NOTES

Opened: 1874
Closed: 1971
Reopened: 1976
Ownership:
    Minehead Railway
    Great Western Railway
    British Railways
    West Somerset Railway
Platforms: One
Signal box: Yes
Toilets: No
Cafe: No
Shop: No
Platform access: Easy –level access to platform

THE SOMERSET & DORSET RAILWAY TRUST

The SDRT came to the West Somerset following the collapse of the Radstock Project, an attempt to bring trains back to part of the old Somerset & Dorset line. Having moved in at Washford, the Trust laid track, put up buildings and established a restoration base and museum dedicated to the much missed S&D. The Trust's largest single possession is 7F 2-8-0 No 88, which has been working trains on the West Somerset since 1987. Opening times depend on the availability of volunteers, but the contact phone number is 01984 640869.

Diesel multiple units have run on the West Somerset from the start of 'preservation era' services back in 1976 and still work on more lightly loaded services during the main timetable periods. Their excellent views of the scenery, particularly if you can get a seat behind the driver, are a well-appreciated feature, and here we see a Class 115/117 unit at Washford. *Sam Burton*

WASHFORD TO BLUE ANCHOR

Having climbed inland to reach Washford, the route now descends towards the sea once more. The descent begins with a curve in a cutting on the steepest part of the West Somerset, which poses a challenge to heavily loaded trains from Minehead to Bishops Lydeard, particularly on damp days when the rails are slippery. As the train runs out of the cutting and on to an embankment, one of the straightest sections of the whole line, it passes over the Monks Path, a footpath once used by the monks and laity from Cleeve Abbey. Just to confuse things, changes to drainage since medieval times mean that much of the year the path also doubles as a stream. As the gradient eases, Exmoor can be seen on the down side, while on the up side the Bristol Channel reappears, together with the camps and caravan parks of Blue Anchor. A curve takes the train into the station.

Right: It does sometimes snow on the Bristol Channel coast. Great Western 'Large Prairie' No 4160 runs around its train during a 'Santa Special' duty in December 2010. *Sam Burton*

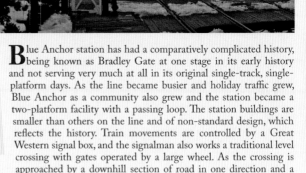

STATION NOTES

Opened: 1904
Closed: 1971
Reopened: 1976
Ownership:
    Great Western Railway
    British Railways
    West Somerset Railway
Platforms: Two
Signal box: Yes
Toilets: No
Cafe: No
Shop: No
Platform access: Narrow – shallow ramps

Blue Anchor station has had a comparatively complicated history, being known as Bradley Gate at one stage in its early history and not serving very much at all in its original single-track, single-platform days. As the line became busier and holiday traffic grew, Blue Anchor as a community also grew and the station became a two-platform facility with a passing loop. The station buildings are smaller than others on the line and of non-standard design, which reflects the history. Train movements are controlled by a Great Western signal box, and the signalman also works a traditional level crossing with gates operated by a large wheel. As the crossing is approached by a downhill section of road in one direction and a sharp turn off the seafront in the other, the road traffic control part of the job is not that easy. The small waiting room on the down platform is now the Railway Museum of the West Somerset Steam Railway Trust, open on Sundays and Bank Holidays when train are running, and during Galas.

The station exits directly on to the seafront, and a right turn takes the visitor for a walk that will provide places to eat and drink. Look to the left and North Hill is clearly visible; it stands behind Minehead and is where Exmoor reaches the Bristol Channel.

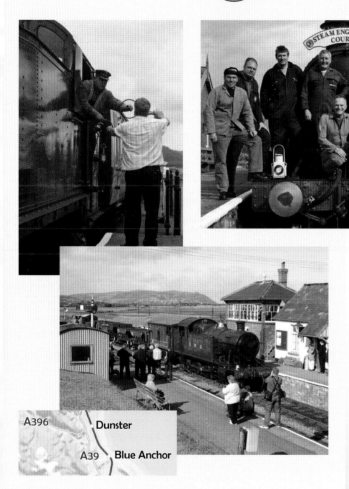

Above left: Token exchange between fireman and signalman as an up train arrives from Minehead. *Ian Smith*

Above right: Footplate Experience Courses are a popular part of the West Somerset's itinerary, and here participants and instructors pose for a photo at the front end of No 9351. *WSR Collection*

Left: GWR heavy freight tank engine No 4247 makes a guest appearance during a Gala and hauls a ballast train over the level crossing and into the station. *Keith Smith*

BLUE ANCHOR TO DUNSTER

O ver this section of the journey the nature of the line changes completely. As the train leaves Blue Anchor it passes a line of three Camping Coaches on the down side, which are now used exclusively for volunteer accommodation. On the up side is the shingle ridge and the beach, which runs to Minehead, a typical Bristol Channel mixture of sand, sediments and pebbles. Running along the coastal plane Exmoor's hills begin to close in. The Conygar Tower – a folly – is ahead on a hill outside Dunster on the down side; the much more venerable Dunster Castle can be seen dominating the village, although sometimes harder to spot against the backdrop of hills. Also on this section the train passes over a wide concrete trough; this is the relief channel for the River Avill, intended to clear water after a spell of rain, but speculation arises as to its purpose after dry spells. The train passes over a level crossing and arrives at Dunster station.

Right: Rather older than the West Somerset Railway, Dunster Castle has stood above its village for more than 1,000 years and is today in the care of the National Trust. It is a popular destination for WSR passengers who can either take the 20-25-minute walk from the station or arrive via the coach link from the popular 'Dunster Castle Express' trains.
Steve Guscott

Bottom right: Great Western '64xx' Class pannier tank No 6430 stands at Dunster station with an 'auto-train' passenger working during a Gala. For three decades classmate No 6412 was based on the line before its owner, the West Somerset Railway Association, sold it to the South Devon Railway to part-fund purchase of No 7821 *Ditcheat Manor.*
Sam Burton

This is another Minehead Railway building, a model of which was the country station in the Hornby model railway range for many years. The goods yard is now home to the Permanent Way Department and track components are usually stacked up here. The goods shed is reputedly haunted.

Dunster village is a gentle uphill walk of about 20 minutes from the station – it has medieval origins, and rewards the effort. Apart from the Castle, now in the care of the National Trust, the visitor can also see the packhorse bridge, an interesting church, parts of a priory and the Yarn Market building. Tearooms, restaurants and pubs abound.

DUNSTER TO MINEHEAD

The last section of the journey is across coastal marshland. Almost immediately after leaving Dunster station the sewage works is passed on the down side, and shortly afterwards the Butlins Holiday Centre appears on the up. The train passes over the Seaward Way level crossing and arrives at the line's northern terminus, Minehead.

DUNSTER

Minehead

A396
Dunster

STATION NOTES

Opened: 1874
Closed: 1971
Reopened: 1976
Ownership:
   Minehead Railway
   Great Western Railway
   British Railways
   West Somerset Railway
Platforms: One
Signal box: Yes
Toilets: No
Cafe: No
Shop: No
Platform access: Easy – level access to platform

MINEHEAD

A seaside terminus, the station is now the Company headquarters.

Facilities for the visitor include the Turntable Café, which as the name suggests stands besides the newly installed turntable. Originally acquired from Pwllheli in the 1970s, a site was finally made available as part of the town's seafront enhancement scheme in the first decade of this century. The table itself was lengthened, the pit created and the track layout altered, and finally it was possible to turn engines at Minehead for the first time since the original locomotive shed was demolished in the early 1960s. The original shed was located in what is now the car park outside the station, and when the line re-opened the Locomotive Department moved into the former goods shed, which has subsequently been extended in a style in keeping with its listed building status. At the far end of the site a more modern shed is used for carriage overhaul and maintenance.

Left: Flower beds, water tower and Class 25 diesel No 7612 at Minehead. *WSR Collection*

Left: 'A1' 'Pacific' No 60163 *Tornado* is one of the best-known steam locomotives following its construction through the 1990s and early 2000s, and it has visited the West Somerset on a number of occasions, attracting large crowds to see and travel behind it. Here *Tornado* arrives at Minehead as the signalman returns to his box after accepting the single-line token for the section from Blue Anchor. *Sam Burton*

STATION NOTES

Opened: 1874
Closed: 1971
Reopened: 1976
Ownership:
  Minehead Railway
  Great Western Railway
  British Railways
  West Somerset Railway
Platforms: Two
Signal box: Yes
Toilets: Yes RADAR
Cafe: Yes
Shop: Yes
Platform access: Level and easy access to platforms

The main station building is another Minehead Railway example, but has been extended and modified over the years. Today the booking office stands facing the seafront, and contains internal fittings from Cardiff General (now Cardiff Central) station. The Buffer Stop shop carries a full range of WSR souvenirs together with books, DVDs, toys and models.

The large size of the platform at Minehead and the area under the canopy means that a variety of open-air events can be held there. The two most regular are the Toy

Top: With North Hill forming a backdrop, No 7828 *Norton Manor 40 Commando* (renamed from *Odney Manor* to mark the WSR's close relations with its neighbours at Norton Manor Camp) shunts into Platform 2 at Minehead station. The footplate crew are obviously enjoying a verbal exchange with the signalman. *Sam Burton*

Middle: A view of Minehead from the peace and quiet of the Old Town on North Hill, away from the bustle of the seaside town below it. The Butlins Pavilion dominates the distant view while the more venerable tower of St Michael's Church is closer to the photographer. *Sam Burton*

Bottom: The WSR has held a number of gala events based on the anniversaries of closure of the much-missed Somerset & Dorset line, which closed in March 1966. During the 2006 Spring Gala a typical S&D express working was recreated with the arrival at Minehead of BR Standard 4MT 'Mogul' No 76079 and Bulleid 'Battle of Britain' 'Pacific' No 34067 *Tangmere*, bringing back memories of a time when this combination of loco classes would appear at Bournemouth West. *Claire Rickson*

and Train Collectors Fair, which usually takes place at the start of the summer holidays, and the Campaign for Real Ale Beer Festival, generally held on the second weekend in September. The station has also been used for filming on a number of occasions, including *Antiques Roadshow* and *The House of Elliott*.

Under the canopy, 'Readers Halt' sells a wide variety of second-hand books and magazines and other goods, the money raised going towards the upkeep of the station.

The beach and promenade are directly opposite the station. Walking straight onwards towards North Hill takes you to the harbour, while a climb up the hill itself takes you to the Old Town. A right turn leads along the front towards Butlins and the Golf Course, while to the left are the shops and town centre. There are plenty of places to eat and drink, as you would expect of a resort town.

MINEHEAD

WHAT TO SEE AND DO NEARBY

Today's passenger arriving at Minehead has a choice of directions and destinations to follow from the station entrance. A left turn across the adjacent car park brings you to the Minehead Eye; this exciting and innovative project provides a dedicated, purpose-built extreme sports skate park and youth centre. A right turn takes you along the seafront towards Butlins Resort. The path continues past the centre and the golf course and can be followed to Dunster Beach and Blue Anchor.

Passengers looking for the beach have simply to cross the road, and there it is.

Crossing the road and walking along the esplanade takes you towards the tall feature of North Hill. Along the way you pass the start of the South West Coast Path, which if followed in its entirety will take you to Poole Harbour via Land's End in Cornwall. The road eventually reaches the harbour, where historic ships the *Waverley* and the *Balmoral* pay their periodic visits to the town, bringing loads of visitors (and some passengers to the Railway) in an evocation of the great days of Bristol Channel shipping. For those seeking some quiet and tranquillity, turning off the esplanade and up into North Hill is recommended, but be aware that there is some hard hill-climbing involved.

The left turn out of the station takes you past the Beach Hotel, popular with coach companies as a base for touring the area, and into the main shopping area of the town. Here there is the usual mixture of seaside souvenir shops and the more specialised outlets, the latter being further from the seafront.

As you would expect, there is a variety of accommodation to suit all pockets in Minehead, and apart from the railway journey it is a good base to explore Exmoor and the Quantock Hills.

Top: The busy platform at Minehead is seen from the footplate of a GWR pannier tank locomotive. *Sam Burton*

Left: An atmospheric picture of British Railways No 70000 *Britannia* moving in the Minehead locomotive shed yard with its cylinder drain cocks open. This 'Pacific' locomotive was the first of 999 different 'Standard' Class locomotives built by BR after nationalisation in 1948. *Sam Burton*

BRIDGES & VIADUCTS

There are no major viaducts on the West Somerset, but there are plenty of bridges, both under and over the line. The highest is at the hamlet of Nethercott between Bishops Lydeard and Crowcombe Heathfield, where the line passes over the lane, and the best known are those over the main roads at Watersmeet, opposite Cedar Falls Health Farm, the pair in the village of Combe Florey, and that at Castle Hill on the outskirts of Williton.

Right: Trains passing under bridges while working hard often produce spectacular effects for photographers, and here Great Western Railway 'King' Class No 6024 *King Edward I* demonstrates the point. *WSR Collection*

Bottom right: The long lens foreshortens the picture and accentuates the curvature of the points as Class 47 No D1661 *North Star* tops the climb from Bishops Lydeard. This is one of the fleet of main-line 'heritage' diesel locomotives in the care of the Williton-based Diesel & Electric Preservation Group. *WSR Collection*

KEEPING THE TRAINS RUNNING: THE RAILWAY DEPARTMENTS...

The West Somerset Railway is an unusual company in that the workforce is made up of a mixture of paid staff and a very large number of volunteers. There are nearly 900 of the latter; some can be seen on the Railway two or three times a week in various roles, while others make weekly or monthly visits to assist. Whatever job they do, they are working in one of the Departments that make up the Railway as a whole and have received the appropriate training.

FRIENDS OF STATIONS

A number of the stations along the route have individual 'Friends of' groups, who carry out maintenance, raise funds and generally assist in making the stations attractive and welcoming to passengers and visitors. Those who have 'Friends of' groups usually advertise this fact and will be happy to talk to you if you wish to help.

THE WEST SOMERSET RAILWAY ASSOCIATION

The West Somerset Railway Association has been the main support body for the WSR right from the start of the project and today has some 5,000 members. Many of these are active volunteers working in the various departments of the Railway, but far more are 'armchair' members who receive an award-winning quarterly magazine and support the Railway by helping with appeals, raffle sales, etc. To find out more contact 01823 433856 or ask for a membership leaflet at one of our stations.

Left: Fortunately station maintenance and train operation rarely have to take place in conditions like these in a part of the world where snow is rare. This is Crowcombe Heathfield, showing the conditions in which the WSR was able to run a full programme of Christmas trains in December 2010. *Alan Turner*

BADGERS MOVE HOME...

As you would expect in an area like West Somerset and Taunton Deane, lineside plants and animal life thrive. The Railway strives to manage its surroundings sensitively, but sometimes unusual problems arise including one in the 1990s when a badger sett began to cause undermining in an embankment. The necessary permissions were obtained and the badgers were relocated to a new home.

PERMANENT WAY

This is the long-established term for the track and infrastructure over which the trains run, and a Department where the volunteer soon learns just how heavy and solidly constructed railway components are. (During TV's *Ground Force*, many were the sardonic smiles on the faces of 'P.Way' staff as disciples of Charlie Dimmock purchased second-hand railway sleepers and discovered the hard way the value of a behind-the-scenes BBC muscle gang to move them about!) However, for those who like the idea of plenty of fresh air and cardio-vascular exercise, this is certainly an invaluable job and a good way of getting toned-up.

CUTTING BACK

This is another Department for those who like fresh air and exercise. As you will have witnessed, there are superb views from WSR trains, but being able to see them depends on keeping lineside growth under control. This is an area where growth is very strong, as you will see if you visit the line in March, after the regular visit of the rail-mounted flails, and compare it with the state of the trackside at the end of August. Cutting back takes place outside the breeding season for local wildlife and is done with an eye on conservation.

Right: The work of the permanent way maintenance gangs, both paid and volunteer, goes on all year round and all along the line. This is track relaying taking place between Blue Anchor and Dunster.

Far right: Concentrating hard to empty the correct amount of ballast from a hopper wagon.

Bottom right: The rail-mounted digger is put to good use during the relaying work. *All Sam Burton*

ON-TRAIN CATERING

Working on the buffet cars is a job where you can be sure of meeting the wide cross-section of the public who make up the passengers on the WSR. The buffet crews usually do two round trips over the whole of the line and sell hot and cold drinks, sandwiches, pasties, snacks and the like. The job does involve a lot of standing, and of course cash handling is involved. Volunteers also assist in the Turntable Café at Minehead.

Below: Britannia first visited the WSR in 1996, and worked trains on two separate visits in 2011. *Sam Burton*

Above left: Some of the offerings available from the buffet cars on the regular service trains, complete with a tempting bottle of locally brewed ale from Wiveliscombe. *Steve Sagrott*

Left: A full train crew for a diesel multiple unit: driver, ticket inspectors, guard and buffet attendant. *Alan Meade*

BOOKING OFFICES

These are part of the Commercial Department and can be very hectic at Bishops Lydeard and Minehead, but quieter at the intermediate stations. Cash handling and reconciliation are key parts of the job, of course, but there is also a need to be able to answer questions about the trains and the places along the way, including some very odd ones! Again, this is a job that will appeal to those who like meeting people.

Right: Welcome to sunny Minehead! Fortunately passengers approaching the station entrance and the booking office do not usually have these weather conditions to negotiate. The original station booking office was in the centre of the main building, but with this area now given over to administration office space, the current booking office was built by the WSR. The interior incorporates parts of the former booking office at Cardiff General (now Cardiff Central).
Martin Snell

Right: The interior of a traditional booking office, in this case at Crowcombe Heathfield with the ticket rack containing the 'Edmondson' tickets clearly visible.
Tim Stanger

Left: The interior of Blue Anchor signal box showing the lever frame, which operates the signals and points, and the large wheel that operates the traditional level crossing gates outside. The cloth on the lever is traditional; by holding it the signalman prevents the well-burnished tops of the levers from becoming tarnished, and maintains the traditionally immaculate working environment. *WSR Collection*

SIGNALLING

The signalman in his signal box has a key responsibility in the safe working of the Railway and control of the trains to keep things moving along our 20 miles of route. On most days of operation the Minehead signalman is also the Controller, the first point of contact and response if there is a problem on the line. Signalmen sometimes spend quite a bit of their duty on their own, so they have to be happy with their own company. Signals need maintenance, and there is a volunteer team that tackles this; some of these volunteers have specialist skills, while others perform more general tasks, wielding shovels and paintbrushes.

I see no ships? Signal maintenance can involve the use of binoculars to check for hand signals from colleagues some considerable distance down the line *Peter Winstanley*

Top: The turntable at Minehead in action, with a large crowd watching and recording how two men can turn a large steam locomotive and tender. *Sam Burton*

Below: Three portraits of locomen at rest, and looking back for the guard's signal to depart. *Dave Rynolds/ Sam Burton (2)*

STATION STAFF

Here is another job that involves plenty of contact with visitors and passengers, making sure that everyone arriving and leaving the station by whatever means does so safely. Staff must also make sure that everything is clean and tidy, liaise with the train crews, and generally assist in the daily running of the Railway. Quite a number of the stations offer some form of catering, and assistance is needed with this, while Minehead station staff also work in the main office handling telephone calls to the Railway and dealing with postal ticket bookings.

LOCOMOTIVE DEPARTMENT

Progress to becoming a steam locomotive driver follows a tried-and-trusted route with training given at each stage. Volunteers begin as cleaners, progress to firemen and eventually become drivers. The speed of this progress depends on aptitude (there is a lot more to being a fireman, for example, than simply shovelling coal) and the number of turns that can be done.

The drivers of the former main-line diesel locomotives are largely drawn from the ranks of the Diesel & Electric Group, and have to be qualified to be able to drive each individual class of loco.

Left: Once the firebox has been raked out, the ash has to be dug out from the pit and taken away for disposal, regardless of rain, frost, wind or blazing sunshine. It is not all glamorous being a driver or a fireman on a steam railway. *Peter Townsend*

Left: Great Western 'Manor' Class No 7821 *Ditcheat Manor* has been purchased by the West Somerset Railway Association but is awaiting the start of overhaul. Pending the commencement of this work the locomotive can be seen at STEAM Museum in Swindon, to which it is on loan. *Peter Townsend*

Bottom left: Danger – men at work! While awaiting the arrival of another train scheduled to pass theirs at Crowcombe Heathfield, the driver, fireman, trainee fireman and guard take the chance to relax and enjoy their surroundings. *Alan Meade*

HOW TO VOLUNTEER

Volunteering your time to help the Railway - Preserving the Past for the Future

Individual enquiries and applications are always welcomed at any time. These should be directed to Mel Hillman, New Volunteer Co-ordinator, The Railway Station, Bishops Lydeard, TA4 3BX, telephone 01823 433856 or email: wsravoltrac@btconnect.com.

Lots of different skills are required. As a prospective new volunteer you could experience supervised work training in any of the following disciplines:

- Signalman
- Station duties
- Booking Clerk
- Draw tickets
- Retail
- Guard
- Travelling Ticket Inspector (TTI)
- Trackside
- Locomotive
- Locomotive restoration
- Catering
- Publicity
- Permanent way gang
- 'Quantock Belle' dining train
- Restoration and Maintenance Squad (RAMS)
- Signal & Telegraph (S&T)

GUARDS AND TRAVELLING TICKET INSPECTORS

The guard is the person in charge of the train and carries the responsibility for its safe operation and the safety of the passengers and the on-train crew. It is therefore a role that requires an overseeing ability and also the capacity to think clearly and decisively if a problem should arise. There is also a need from time to time to carry out shunting. The Travel Ticketing Inspector's prime role is that of revenue protection, checking tickets and selling them to any passengers who have been unable to buy one before boarding the train. They also work with the guards to ensure the safe operation of the train and to make sure that passengers board and alight safely and at the right station. As another point of contact, the TTI can expect to have to answer a variety of questions through the day.

Above right: Right away! *Sam Burton*

Far right: "All Aboard!"

Right: Connecting the vacuum pipes *Alan Meade*

SHOPS BY STATION

The two main shops are at Bishops Lydeard and Minehead, but all the stations except Doniford Halt have sales counters. That at Washford specialises in publications relating to the Somerset & Dorset Joint Railway.

THE BUFFER STOP SHOP

The Buffer Stop Shop has a full range of specialist books, DVDs and magazines available for the enthusiast. For the modeller it stocks a range of Hornby and Bachmann railway sets and accessories.

Do you need to keep warm? A colourful range of West Somerset Railway clothing can be purchased, including fleece jackets, sweatshirts, rugby shirts, T-shirts, hats and all manner of other items.

We also have local interest books, DVDs, postcards, greetings cards and postage stamps, souvenir tea-towels, calendars, china, fridge magnets, key rings – and much, much more!

Not forgetting the younger visitor, we stock an extensive selection of 'Thomas and Friends' merchandise, including the 'Take Along Thomas' range, toys, books, playsets and individual models.

The Buffer Stop Shop attracts business both from WSR passengers and from visitors to the town, and the range of goods stocked is aimed at attracting both markets Book launches and signings, such as those shown here *(above)* featuring David Williams and John Parsons are a regular part of the calendar. *All WSR Collection*

Bishops Lydeard

The Whistle Stop Café On Platform 2 adjacent to the signal box, The Whistle-stop Café sells hot and cold snack items as well as a soft drinks and sweets.

Stogumber

Refreshment Room (the old station office). Here you can also partake of one of the station's now famous cream teas. On gala days bacon rolls, sausage rolls and pasties are always popular, and in colder weather tea and crumpets are served.

Minehead

The Turntable Café offers a wide menu including a selection of sandwiches, hot food, chilled items, cakes, biscuits, confectionery and snacks. The Turntable Café offers a range of freshly made speciality coffees and teas, not forgetting our best-selling mugs of original tea and filter coffee.

Food is fresh and where possible locally sourced. All sandwiches and rolls are freshly made each day. We offer the choice of a fast-track takeaway service or a more leisurely eat-in experience.

WSR Collection

THE WEST SOMERSET STEAM RAILWAY TRUST

Another long-standing group, the Steam Trust's main role is to conserve and preserve items of historic interest for future generations. It has a small Museum at Blue Anchor station and has helped to fund steam locomotive restoration for the line. However, the Trust's major ongoing project is the Heritage Carriages Fund, which has acquired and begun to restore a number of Great Western Railway carriages. The first was a sleeping car dating from 1897, which had spent many years as part of a bungalow at Stogursey. By its nature this is not a vehicle for daily service, but can usually be viewed in the Gauge Museum at Bishops Lydeard. However, other vehicles now being tackled as finance, time and skill permits should see service on special occasions. Former GWR coach No 6705 has been repatriated from the USA, and after much initial restoration work was carried out at Crewe has now been moved to Williton for completion. The Trust's headquarters is at Williton station.

TAKING CARE OF OUR HERITAGE

MAINTENANCE AND PAINTING

Most of the stations carry out their own routine maintenance and painting work, much of it carried out in the late autumn, winter and early spring when trains are fewer, and they welcome anyone with good DIY abilities. There is also a team based at Bishops Lydeard that assists with larger projects along the line.

Steam locomotives have carried names and numbers right from the start, even if some of the earliest crews would not have been able to read them. These two photographs show part of the interior of Minehead's loco shed with the final fettling up and fitting of Great Western cab-side number plates and name plates for No 6960 *Raveningham Hall*.
Sam Burton

Steam locomotive stock list*

Loco No	Class	Wheel Arr	Designer/Builder	Year built	Weight
Ex-Great Western Railway					
3850	2800	2-8-0	Churchward/Collett, Swindon	1942	76 tons 5 cwt
4160	5101 4MT	2-6-2T	Churchward/Collett, Swindon	1948	78 tons 9 cwt
4561	4500 4MT	2-6-2T	Churchward, Swindon	1924	57 tons
5553	4500 4MT	2-6-2T	Churchward, Swindon	1928	61 tons
6960 *Raveningham Hall*	6959 5MT	4-6-0	Hawkesworth, Swindon	1944	75 tons 16cwt
West Somerset Railway					
9351	Mogul	2-6-0	*Collett*, Minehead	2000-4	
Ex- Southern Railway					
34046 *Braunton*	Rebuilt West Country	4-6-2	Bullied, Brighton	1946	86 tons
Ex- London Midland & Scottish Railway					
Ex-London North Eastern Railway					
Ex-Somerset & Dorset Joint Railway					
88 (BR No: 53808)	7F	2-8-0	Fowler, Darlington	1925	64 tons 15 cwt
Ex-British Railways					
7820 *Dinmore Manor*	7800 5MT	4-6-0	Collett, Swindon	1950	68 tons 18 cwt
7821 *Ditcheat Manor*	7800 5MT	4-6-0	Collett, Swindon	1950	68 tons 18 cwt
7828 *Odney Manor (BR) Norton Manor (WSR)*	7800 5MT	4-6-0	Collett, Swindon	1950	68 tons 18 cwt
Ex-Army					
Ex-Industrial Locos					
Kilmersdon (Saddle Tank)		0-4-0	Peckett, Bristol	1929	

* Please note that the above listing and that of diesels on page XLII are made up of locomotives normally based on the WSR and as at the time of writing. However throughout the year additional visiting locomomotives are often to be seen on the railway. Locomotives from the WSR also visit other locations for galas, events or overhaul.

Top left: Great Western 'Small Prairie' locomotives have served the line in Great Western, British Railways and WSR days since at least the 1920s. No 5553 has left the line for overhaul and work is going ahead with the overhaul of sister loco No 4561 at Williton. No 5553 is the personal property of Pete Waterman, and is on long-term hire to the WSR. *Peter Townsend*

Middle: No 3850 is a GWR '2884' Class heavy freight locomotive built at Swindon in 1942, and has been purchased and restored by its owning group, Dinmore Manor Locomotive Ltd, which also owns three other locomotives. It is the most powerful steam engine on the line, easily able to cope with the heaviest trains. *Peter Townsend*

Bottom: No 4160 is also privately owned by a group. Built to a Great Western design in March 1948, just after the nationalisation of the railways, it is a 'Large Prairie' and a surviving example of a class that mainly worked heavy suburban and main-line stopping trains. Examples of the class were seen on the Minehead line in GWR and BR days. *Peter Townsend*

Top: Resplendent in the Prussian Blue livery of the Somerset & Dorset Joint Railway, No 88 was originally built to work heavy freight trains over the Mendip Hills. It is now owned by the Washford-based Somerset & Dorset Railway Trust, and is one of two survivors of an original class strength of 11. *Peter Townsend*

Middle: Intended for express passenger work over secondary main lines such as that of the Cambrian section in Mid Wales, the 'Manors' are ideal for the preservation-era WSR. Built at Swindon in 1950 as *Odney Manor*, No 7828 was renamed *Norton Manor 40 Commando* in honour of the Railway's neighbours at Norton Fitzwarren. Sister engine No 7820 *Dinmore Manor* is being overhauled before returning to the WSR, and No 7821 *Ditcheat Manor* is owned by the West Somerset Railway Association, but is on display at STEAM Museum in Swindon. *WSR Collection*

Bottom: No 34046 *Braunton* is a rebuilt Bulleid 'West Country' 'light Pacific' of a type that worked express trains across the Southern Region of BR from Dover to Devon. Owned by Mr Jeremy Hoskins, the locomotive will divide its time between peak-period services on the WSR and main-line excursion work. *Alan Meade*

Top: Designed by the Great Western in the 1930s but not built until the 1990s, when the WSR decided to see what the proposed engine could do if it was brought to life, No 9351 is a unique machine that has proved a versatile and valuable locomotive since it entered traffic. It is a smaller-boilered version of the GWR 'Moguls', which were once a common sight on the lines from Taunton to Barnstaple and Ilfracombe, and to Minehead. *Alan Meade*

Middle: No 4561, currently being overhauled by West Somerset Restoration at Williton (and not on public view), is one of the 'Small Prairie' tank engines that were the mainstay of Great Western and British Railways (Western Region) branch-line services from the 1910s to the end of steam in the 1960s. *Alan Meade*

Bottom: Kilmersdon was the last steam engine to work in industry in Somerset, working at Kilmersdon Colliery in the North Somerset coalfield until it closed at the beginning of the 1970s. It is one of many rugged, small saddle tank engines built for industrial use by Peckett of Bristol, and is in the care of the Somerset & Dorset Railway Trust at Washford. It assumes the identity of 'Percy' during 'Thomas' events. *Steve Sagrott*

THE DIESEL AND ELECTRIC PRESERVATION GROUP

Staunch supporters of the WSR through good and bad times the DEPG were one of the first groups to act when the first generation of British Railways diesel locomotives were being superseded at the start of the 1970's and in danger of vanishing into history leaving no extant examples behind them. The first acquisitions were diesel hydraulics from the Western Region but the Williton based collection now has a wide range of types available for traffic and under restoration. Their base is normally open at weekends and you can expect a friendly reception if you would like to know more.

Above: Class 04 No D2271 and Class 03 No D2133 stand together between shunting jobs at Minehead. D2133 has never worked outside Somerset in its 50-year existence, being allocated to Taunton loco shed when new. From there it was sold to British Celanese as a works shunter at Bridgwater, and when that large works was closing down the engine was presented to the WSR. *Peter Townsend*

Diesel Locomotive Stock List

Loco No	Class	Wheel Arr	Builder	Year built	Weight
Ex-British Railways					
D1010 *Western Campaigner*	52	C-C	British Railways Swindon works	1962	108 tons
D832 *Onslaught*	42	B-B	British Railways Swindon works	1958	78 tons
D7017	35	B-B	Beyer Peacock, Manchester	1962	74 tons
D7018 †	35	B-B	Beyer Peacock, Manchester	1962	74 tons
D9526	14	0-6-0	British Railways Swindon works	1964	49 tons 6 cwt
D9518 †	14	0-6-0	British Railways Swindon works	1964	49 tons 6 cwt
D6566	33	Bo-Bo	Bimingham Carriage & Wagon Co	1961	74 tons 4 cwt
D6575 †	33	Bo-Bo	Bimingham Carriage & Wagon Co	1961	74 tons 4 cwt
D1661 *North Star*	47	Co-Co	British Railways Crewe works	1965	127 tons
D2133	03	0-6-0	British Railways Swindon works	1960	30 tons 16 cwt
D2271	04	0-6-0	Robert Stephenson & Hawthorn	1958	29 tons 15 cwt
D3462	08	0-6-0	British Railways Darlington works	1957	48 tons 0 cwt

† denotes locomotive undergoing overhaul or restoration as at February 2012.

Top: Class 47 No D1661 *North Star* is one of a number of this very successful class of diesel-electric locomotives that were allocated when new to the Western Region of BR and were given names of famous Great Western Railway steam engines. It is seen here at Minehead. *Claire Rickson*

Middle: Class 42 'Warship' diesel-hydraulic No D832 *Onslaught* was one of a class of 71 diesel-hydraulic express locomotives built for the Western Region, and is one of only two surviving members of the type. Fast and powerful, the 'Warships' were condemned to a short working life by virtue of being non-standard machines as British Railways settled on electric rather than hydraulic transmission systems. *Sam Burton*

Bottom: British Railways Class 52 No D1010 *Western Campaigner* is the most powerful diesel-hydraulic locomotive owned by the Diesel & Electric Preservation Group, and a very popular locomotive with enthusiasts who remember these express engines in their pomp in the 1960s and '70s at the head of such trains as the 'Golden Hind' and 'Cornish Riviera'. *WSR Collection*

SPECIAL EVENTS

- Steam Engineman Course
- Diesel Experience Course
- Snow Drops and Steam
- Spring Steam Gala
- Watchet 150 (in 2012)
- West Somerset Mineral Line Trips
- 'The Quantock Belle' 1st Class Dining Train
- 'Dunster Castle Express'
- Exmoor Day Out by Steam Train and Classic Coach
- 'Hestercombe Express'
- Murder Mystery Specials
- Mixed Traction Weekend
- Day Out With Thomas™
- Fish and Chip Special
- Cheese and Cider Specials
- Steam and Cream Special
- Minehead Toy & Train Fair
- Steam Fayre and Vintage Vehicle Rally
- Late Summer Weekend
- CAMRA Real Ale Festival
- Autumn Steam Gala
- Santa Express and Santa Specials
- Dunster By Candlelight
- Carol Trains
- Winter Steam Festival

THEMED TRAINS

The core of the Railway's business is its 200-days-a-year train operation, but this is augmented by special workings for those who are looking for something 'extra' or just a little different. 'Murder Mystery' trains offer a chance to exercise the 'little grey cells' to solve the murder resulting from the scenes played out before you on the journey. Fish and Chip Specials, Steam and Cream, and Cider and Cheese are also popular parts of the annual programme.

SANTA SPECIALS

The Santa trains run at weekends and other selected dates from early December up to and including Christmas Eve. 'Santa Expresses' operate from Bishops Lydeard, with Santa walking through the train with his helpers, while 'Santa Specials' run from Bishops Lydeard and Minehead to visit the man in the red suit at his grottos at Crowcombe Heathfield and

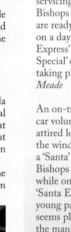

Blue Anchor respectively. The fares include the train journey, a present for each child and some seasonal refreshments for the adults.

GALAS

The West Somerset Railway's Gala events are a popular part of the annual diary for many enthusiasts and also a great day out for the general public who want to see a wide selection of locomotives in action.

The Spring Steam Gala is one of the major events of its kind and has grown

Top right: It is not permitted for members of the public to climb up the signal gantry at Minehead, but this picture taken, from that rather precarious spot by a WSR worker, shows photographers capturing an up train leaving behind 'guest' engine No 30777 *Sir Lamiel* during the 2011 Spring Steam Gala. *Sam Burton*

to the point where it takes place over the last two weekends of March (barring an early Easter), with the second weekend also incorporating the preceding Thursday and Friday. Apart from benefiting the Railway, this Gala also brings welcome early-season trade to many local accommodation providers.

The Mixed Traffic Weekend is three days when the WSR works virtually all of its trains using vintage diesel locomotives, many being from the DEPG collection at Williton, and with the diesel-hydraulic machines of the former Western Region of British Railways very evident. This Gala usually takes place in mid-June.

The Autumn Steam Gala is a four-day event that takes place at the juncture of September and October, and is another major treat for all lovers of the steam locomotive.

All three of these major events feature trade stands and other attractions to augment the intensive train services, and 'guest' locomotives are hired from other heritage railways to augment the home-based fleets.

The Late Summer Weekend takes place on the first weekend in September and features a mixture of steam and vintage diesel locomotives, mostly drawn from the home fleet but with some guest appearances taking place. Similarly, the Winter Steam Festival, which takes place on two days between Christmas and New Year is mainly concerned with WSR-based engines, but a guest does appear from time to time.

Bottom right: During the same event a picture taken from the windows of Bishops Lydeard signal box shows another 'guest' locomotive, No 70000 *Britannia*, attracting an admiring crowd, while yet another 'visitor', pannier tank No 6430, is carrying out 'auto-train' duties along the line from the station towards Norton Fitzwarren. *Ken Davidge*

THEMED TRIPS TO LOCAL ATTRACTIONS

The West Somerset is increasingly working to offer 'more than a train ride', with additional packages on selected dates. There is the 'Dunster Castle Express' twice a week from Bishops Lydeard with a coach link from Dunster station to the Castle for a day out at this 1,000-year-old part of British history. Running on selected dates from the Minehead end of the line, the 'Hestercombe Express' has a coach link to these wonderfully restored formal gardens.

Other popular packages include a steam train ride combined with a 'Mystery Tour' by coach around Exmoor, a day out by train and coach exploring the remains of the West Somerset Mineral Railway, and a new link to visit the Exmoor Pony Centre. The Railway also operates bus links from Dunster station for the annual Country Fair and Dunster Show days.

Above: No 9351, dating from the 1990s, has the 900-years-older castle at Dunster as a backdrop while making its way towards Minehead with a down train. The castle sits on its hill above the attractive medieval village, which is around 20 minutes walking time from the station. *Steve Guscott*

Left: The headboard of the twice-weekly 'Dunster Castle Express' train incorporates the logo of the National Trust, in whose care the castle now is. *Steve Guscott*

Below: This panoramic view shows the curve of Blue Anchor Bay looking towards Blue Anchor station and the railway following the coastline to Dunster and Minehead. The up train leaving the station is about to start the climb inland towards Washford, which includes the steepest gradient on the WSR, a section at 1 in 65. *WSR Collection*

FUN AND GAMES   THE WSR CROSSWORD

Crossword clues:

Across

4 Number of platforms at Crowcombe Heathfield station (3)

8 English ___, organisation that now cares for 10 across Abbey (8)

9 Stops briefly – at a station, perhaps (6)

10 ___ Abbey, historic location reached from Washford station (6)

11 WSR Halt that uses a corrugated iron pagoda shelter from Cove on the Exe Valley line (8)

13 Member of a group supporting a particular station (6)

14 Major London terminus for southern England (8)

15 River whose gorge is spanned by Brunel's Clifton Suspension Bridge (4)

16 Vehicle carrying coal and water for a steam loco (6)

18 Strong and sturdy in construction (6)

21 ___ Anchor, WSR station (4)

22 Booked a seat on a train, perhaps (8)

24 One of the two Bagnall industrial locos that hauled trains in the early years (6)

26 2 down and 11 across, for example (8)

29 Firmly fixed in the ground, like a plant or tree (6)

30 The other Bagnall industrial loco that hauled trains in the early years (6)

31 Lord ___ of Beaulieu, who flagged away the first train from 2 down on 28 March 1976 (8)

32 '2 down ___', innovative skate park and youth centre in the town (3)

Down

1 Underground room for storing wine, perhaps (6)

2 Location of the company headquarters of the WSR (8)

3 Table of days, weeks and months (8)

4 Look after the first syllable of 16 across! (4)

5 Accessible and ready for business (4)

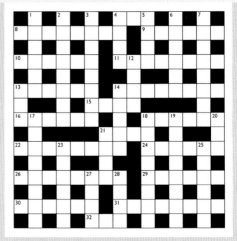

6 '___ Stop', shop at 2 down (6)

7 Places to enjoy a nice cuppa! (8)

12 Fishing port of Western Scotland (4)

13 Like Thomas's Controller? (3)

14 The Earth, its countries and peoples (5)

17 Diesel & ___ Preservation Group, based at Williton (8)

18 Title of Wilbert Awdry, creator of 'Thomas the Tank Engine' (8)

19 Royal castle giving its name to a historic ship that makes occasional visits to 2 down (8)

20 Number of WSR 26 across from Bishops Lydeard and Minehead inclusive (3)

21 Edible seed – kidney or broad, for example (4)

23 Greenway is a housing one outside Bishops Lydeard (6)

25 Road lined with trees (6)

27 Shrek, for example! (4)

28 Not all – but half of Somerset! (4)

Compiled by
Will Adams

SOLUTION

Across: 4 Two 8 Heritage 9 Pauses 10 Cleeve 11 Doniford 13 Friend 14 Waterloo 15 Avon 16 Tender 18 Robust 21 Blue 22 Reserved 24 Vulcan 26 Stations 29 Rooted 30 Victor 31 Montague 32 Eye

Down: 1 Cellar 2 Minehead 3 Calendar 4 Tend 5 Open 6 Buffer 7 Tearooms 12 Oban 13 Fat 14 World 17 Electric 18 Reverend 19 Balmoral 20 Ten 21 Bean 23 Estate 25 Avenue 27 Ogre 28 Some

The WSR Quiz

Q. In what year did the final expansion of the West Somerset Railway occur?

A. ....

Q. When did the branch line from Taunton to Chard close?

A. ....

Q. The Gauge Museum is located in a building previously used as what?

A. ....

Q. At which station is the Gauge Museum located?

A. ....

Q. Which Halt is mentioned in one of Evelyn Waugh's novels?

A. ....

Q. Crowcombe Heathfield has appeared in a number of TV and film productions – can you name one of them mentioned in this guide?

A. ....

Q. Contained within our station (or Halt) names are words that mean other things. Can you find the word and the station name?

1 A measure of weight

Word: ....

Station name: ....

2. A road passing through water

Word: ....

Station names: ....

3. A time piece

Word: ....

Station name: ....

Quick Quiz

Q 1: How many passengers are carried each year on the WSR?

A: More than ....

Q 2: Who looks after Dunster Castle?

A: ....

Q 3: How are the gates at Blue Anchor level crossing operated?

A: ....

Q 4: What is the name of the 1st Class Dining Train?

A: ....

Q 5: What is the name of our shop at Minehead station?

A: ....

4. This is where tin, coal and salt can be found

Word: ....

Station name: ....

5. A place to buy things.

Word: ....

Station name: ....

6. Similar but not a rook or raven!

Word: ....

Station name: ....

Answers: **Quick Quiz:** 1. 200,000 2. The National Trust 3 A large wheel 4. The Quantock Belle 5 The Buffer Stop Shop
The WSR Quiz: 1934 • 1962 • Goods Shed • Bishops Lydeard • Combe Florey Halt • *A Hard Days Night* or *The Land Girls* • 1. Ton/Williton • 2. Ford/Donniford Halt and Washford • 3. Watch/Watchet • 4. Mine/Minehead • 5. Shop/Bishops Lydeard • 6. Crow/Crowcombe Heathfield